YMCA of the Rockies:

Spanning a Century

By

Jack R. Melton

and

Lulabeth Melton

Written under the auspices of the
Lula W. Dorsey Museum, YMCA of the Rockies

*Dedicated to all the
supporters and friends
of the Lula W. Dorsey Museum*

Acknowledgments

Thanking everyone who has contributed to this book in one way or another is impossible, but there are a number who deserve recognition. First and foremost we thank the "string savers" of the world who saved things that were special to them providing details missing in official records of the Association.

Lula W. Dorsey remembered many of the persons and events mentioned in this book, and she knew the importance of preserving the past. Her friend, Walter G. Ruesch, is owed a debt of gratitude by all who enjoy the Dorsey Museum and this book. In 1979 several members of the Board of Directors took us under their wing. Through the years they and many new friends on the Board have continued supporting the museum.

Since 1979 numerous families and individuals have shared their recollections, photographs, mementoes, and made audio tapes. By sharing their love of the YMCA of the Rockies with us, they have enriched our lives and provided insight necessary to write this history.

In November 1991, Jack made a trip to the YMCA of the USA Archives at the University of Minnesota. There, Archivist Andrea Hinding and her staff, David Carmichael and Dagmar Getz, opened many doors.

Alice Wiggins deserves much credit for helping us put the finishing touches on the Guy LaCoste story. She passed along our request for research help in Salt Lake City to Dick Stevens who found a biography of LaCoste.

One of the most important pieces to the Guy LaCoste story was provided by a kindly librarian in the Denver Public Library who helped us locate a photograph of LaCoste. We only wish we had thought to ask her name in the excitement of the moment.

Eric Paddock, Curator of Photography, and Rebecca Lintz, Assistant Director of Collection Services, at the Colorado State Historical Society were invaluable in researching the Clatworthy Collection. Their tolerance of our questions was unending.

Several public libraries including those in the Estes Park, Loveland, Ft. Collins, and Denver were instrumental in providing bits and pieces that filled in many gaps.

Betty Kilsdonk and Susan Ellis of the Grand County Historical Society were helpful in putting together the Middle Park and Just Ranch portions of this book. Grand Lake historian, Patience Kemp, provided valuable insight into Grand Lake at the turn of the century.

The employees of the Larimer County Clerk and Recorders Office deserve recognition for their assistance in unraveling the complicated land dealings of the Earl of Dunraven and Guy LaCoste. Their patience was admirable even when Jack broke one of their microfilm readers.

The story of early Camp Chief Ouray were unraveled through the kindness of Pete Gabel, Vice President of Communications and Financial Development. He allowed us access to the extensive material contained in the files of the Denver YMCA.

Our dear friend Sybil Barnes edited the original manuscript. Her many suggestions were invaluable.Many of our co-workers at the YMCA of the Rockies took time out from their regular duties to help with this book: Gene Garris, Scott Pope, Dave Thomas, Muriel Whiting, Gary Baxter, Ellie Orbison, and Mark Birdseye. Several friends read the manuscript searching for errors: Dave Barclay, Bud Landis, Ruth Tasto, Bert Muse, and Debbie Brewster.

Through the years the unsung heroes of the Dorsey Museum have been our seasonal co-workers. Each of them had a part in making this project a reality. Mary Margret Doak deserves special thanks. Her hard work through the years made researching the museum's archives much easier.

Last, we thank all of those who bought into the vision we had for the Lula W. Dorsey Museum in 1979.

Preface

Each year over 100,000 people are added to the roster of individuals who have used the facilities of the YMCA of the Rockies since 1908. Each individual leaves the YMCA of the Rockies with a unique set of experiences; however, all share a common bond in fulfilling the dreams of the Association's founders and adherents.

Whether you are a first time visitor, an old timer, or staff member, you share the equally impossible task of explaining what the YMCA of the Rockies is to someone who has not experienced it. We hope that this book will help you understand your experiences and share them with others.

Table of Contents

Our YMCA Heritage

YMCA of the Rockies Statement of Purpose:

The Young Men's Christian Association we regard as being, in its essential genius, a worldwide fellowship united by a common loyalty to Jesus Christ for the purpose of developing Christian personality and building a Christian Society. Therefore, the YMCA of the Rockies commits itself to:
- Providing an experience for families in a Christian environment;
- Serving conferences of a religious, educational and recreational nature in a Christian environment;
- Offering a resident camping experience for boys and girls in a Christian environment, and;
- Serving its staff by providing leadership training and a work experience in a Christian organization.

The Beginnings of the YMCA Movement

According to C. Howard Hopkins the YMCA Movement has its foundations within the Protestant Reformation. The evangelical revival and accompanying concern for young men adrift in the English cities led to the founding of the Young Men's Christian Association.

The acknowledged founder of the YMCA was Sir George Williams. Moving to Bridgewater from rural Somerset he was apprenticed to a dry goods merchant. After completing his apprenticeship in 1841, Williams was employed at Hitchock and Rogers as a clerk joining about 140 other young men. The hours were long and the working and living conditions abysmal.

Williams joined the Congregational Church and became active in Sunday School work. Together with some like-minded co-workers Williams began holding prayer meetings at Hitchcock and Rogers. The head of the firm was converted and began supporting the Young Men's Missionary Society. Soon prayer meetings were organized at other firms leading to the founding of the YMCA on June 6, 1844.

The YMCA came to North America in 1851 focusing upon the moral, mental and physical salvation of young men. In North America the Protestant middle class of the cities and small towns quickly embraced the nondenominational Movement. Successive waves of revivalism sweeping the country once every generation since the 1730s embraced the YMCA and carried it forward.

Sir George Williams.
Lula W. Dorsey Museum

The YMCA grew into maturity during the last thirty years of the nineteenth century. It was a time of dynamic change for the United States. The forces of economic and industrial growth combined with the realization of manifest destiny, transformed a largely rural America into a nation of cities.

As the YMCA gained strength and structure, it began to resemble the businesses of the men who were its leaders. The YMCA became institutionalized. Formal organization required formal training. That need formed the basis for the founding of the YMCA of the Rockies.

Tourists Come to Estes Park

With an elevation too high for successful agriculture, no mineral deposits and relative isolation, Estes Park had to find another reason to thrive. That reason was found in catering to the tourists attracted by the area's natural beauty. The first "tourists" were the Ute, Shoshoni, Comanche, and Arapaho using the Valley as a summer hunting ground and refuge from the blazing heat of the plains much like the summer tourists of today.

Early Estes Park Tourism

Even though Longs and Meeker, Les deux Oreilles (The two Ears), were familiar landmarks in the Front Range, most early explorers, cartographers, and military men bypassed the Estes Valley. Spanish explorers came near and may even have seen the Valley. French fur trappers certainly worked the Big Thompson River and its tributaries.

It was not until fall 1843 that the first recorded visit to Estes Park took place. Rufus B. Sage, a native of Connecticut, "discovered" the valley while on a three year journey through the west. Abundant game, lofty peaks, streams, and beautiful solitude enticed him to spend the month of October. After returning home, he wrote a book in which he described the Valley as a place where "he might hold daily converse with himself, Nature, and his God, far removed from the annoyance of man."

In 1860 the valley welcomed its first homesteader. Joel Estes had come west from Missouri after having caught "gold fever" in 1849. The Estes family wandered around the west including California and Oregon until news of gold brought them to Colorado in 1859. While on a hunting or prospecting trip, Joel Estes and son Milton visited the Valley which bears their name. Like Rufus Sage they were enchanted by its beauty. The next year they returned and built two cabins. However, after only six years the Estes family left looking for more suitable climes to pursue ranching.

In 1872 Estes Park was visited by a person who began to change the face of the Valley. That person was Windham Thomas Wyndham-Quinn better known as the Earl of Dunraven. He was drawn to Estes Park by abundant game. The hunting was excellent, but soon the Earl found himself captivated by the natural beauty of the Valley.

At some point, the Earl decided that he wanted all of Estes Park for himself. With the help of Denver bankers and lawyers along with unscrupulous men filing for homesteads, he quickly controlled most of the Valley. Land grabbing by the English Earl ran afoul of other land owners in the area. The resulting disputes are legendary in Estes Park history.

To hold on to the land, the Earl had to find a way to make it self supporting. To do so, he built the Estes Park Hotel in 1877. Located in the eastern edge of the Valley, it catered to a growing tourist trade. Its opening and resulting publicity hastened the transformation of Estes Park from an isolated mountain valley into a tourist mecca.

In 1873 Estes Park was visited by one of its most celebrated tourists, Isabella Bird. In a Lady's Life in the Rocky Mountains, she fondly recalled her three month stay in the Valley. Like tourists before her and countless ones since she described the majesty that surrounded her. Isabella Bird rented a small cabin from the Griff Evans family who made a habit of taking in tourists and were probably the Valley's first innkeepers.

Soon, others arrived with the idea of profiting from the natural beauty of the Valley and the tourists who came. Abner Sprague began feeding hungry travelers in Moraine Park. Elkanah Lamb built Longs Peak House in 1875 and guided tourists up Longs Peak for $5. Mrs. W.E. James opened Elkhorn Lodge in 1877, and H.W. Ferguson built the Highlands. In the early 1880s John Cleave opened a general store. By the turn of the century, catering to the needs of tourists had become a way of life in Estes Park.

Camping out in Estes Park, circa 1876.
Courtesy of Lulabeth and Jack Melton

The Dunraven Hotel.
Courtesy of the Estes Park Area Historical Museum

Elkhorn Lodge in the 1880s.
Courtesy of Lulabeth and Jack Melton

Visionary or Just Another Land Speculator?

In 1899 or 1900 Estes Park was visited by a twenty-five year old French-American entrepreneur whom Anna Wolfrom Dove described as "young, ambitious, and anxious to make some money...." Guy Robert LaCoste was exceedingly handsome with intense penetrating eyes and swarthy countenance. LaCoste, like the Earl of Dunraven, realized that the wealth of Estes Park lay in its natural beauty. It was only waiting to be "mined" by the right person. LaCoste saw a metamorphosis coming that would transform Estes Park into a tourist mecca, and he wanted to be at the nucleus of that change.

Reaching for the Brass Ring

Guy Robert LaCoste was born on March 6, 1875 in Lawrenceville, Pennsylvania into a family who counted General Israel Putnam of the American Revolution and followers of LaFayette among their progenitors. The LaCoste family including parents, Robert and Mary, Guy, and three brothers Fred, William, and Leon moved to Creede, Colorado. There, during the silver boom, they found wealth. In 1890, the elder LaCoste moved his family to Denver where a man could be a millionaire and a pauper and a millionaire again all in the same day. Establishing the Hampton-LaCoste Loan & Investment Company, Robert LaCoste evidently found prosperity in financing others' dreams. Guy grew up in a house where schemes and tales of instantaneous wealth were everyday fare.

After graduation from high school in Denver, Guy LaCoste embarked upon a newspaper career working for the <u>Denver Post</u>, <u>Kansas City Star</u>, and <u>St. Louis Post Dispatch</u>. Returning to Denver in the mid 1890s he continued his newspaper career by working as editor at the <u>Denver Post</u>, reporter at the <u>Denver Republican</u>, and editor of the <u>Denver Times</u>.

After visiting Estes Park, LaCoste realized that land was required to extract the wealth he saw in the Valley. There was precious little left after the Earl of Dunraven and later home-

steaders had snatched up the choicest parcels. La-Coste located 360 acres west of town on which he staked a claim. The parcel was a magnificent gem in the rough stretching eastward from the slopes of Green Mountain (Emerald Mountain) to the babbling waters of Wind River. There were tranquil meadows, heavily forested slopes, and two springs providing "pure, soft mountain water, as cold as ice." Below the springs on the slopes of Emerald Mountain, La-Coste built a small dugout securing his claim. Accord-

Guy Robert LaCoste.
Lula W. Dorsey Museum

ing to Anna Wolfrom Dove, who homesteaded on Wind River in 1907, LaCoste "put his parents there to fulfill the requirements of law necessary, while he continued" his newspaper career.

LaCoste quickly added to his homestead by purchasing additional land. On January 30, 1902 he purchased 320 acres from Charley Hewitt and an additional 320 acres from John Hewitt. LaCoste now owned almost 1000 acres. Next, LaCoste incorporated the Estes Park Land and Investment Company with George D. Sullivan and Arthur B. West on December 16, 1901. The purpose of the Company as stated in the Certificate of Incorporation was:

> ...to buy, sell and lease real estate..., to borrow and loan money..., to give and take mortgages..., to build, construct and maintain hotels, inns and other places of public entertainment..., (and to) carry on the general business of hotel or innkeeper....

The Company's assets included LaCoste's property and $20,000 in working capital. Moving quickly, they built the Wind River Lodge which was ready for operation in the summer of 1902. The Lodge was described as:

> ...a rustic, two-story club house of fourteen rooms, on the edge of a grove of pines. It has wide verandas, a large dining hall, and parlor with a big open fireplace. The lower floor can be thrown into one large room for dancing and entertainments....

The rustic appearance referred to the Lodge's Western Stick architecture characterized by roofs of broad, gentle pitch. Although the Lodge was of frame construction, siding of native ponderosa pine with bark intact gave the effect of a log building. The same wood was used as roofing. Porch posts and railings were made from whole trees adding to the ambiance and carrying out the stick theme.

While developing the Wind River Lodge resort, LaCoste built a more substantial cabin adjoining his dugout. Constructed of full logs, the Western Stick style was again carried out using rustic timber as roofing and siding on the gables. This was a homestead cabin supposedly occupied by the owner. However, since LaCoste maintained a home in Denver, it was probably rented to guests as part of the resort.

The Wind River Lodge complex included six buildings, several tents, and at least one tent cabin. An accurate count and description of all structures is impossible. Due to architectural similarities, it is believed that at least two cabins were constructed at the same time as the Lodge or shortly thereafter. One, a seven room cottage, was described as having "a large living room with fireplace, etc." and carrying out the Western Stick style by being "built in an artistic fashion." It differed from the main Lodge as it was "completely furnished for housekeeping...." Another three room cottage with kitchen was constructed in the same style.

A small, one room cabin on the property may not have been included in the count as it may have served as a manager's or cook's cabin. It differed from the above two in that it was built of full logs; however, Western Stick style was evident in artistically angled siding on the gables and above the door. Two additional cabins from the Wind River Lodge period are believed to have been built after 1902 since both lack the rustic siding.

With hotel rooms, sleeping cabins, and housekeeping cottages, the Wind River Lodge catered to an assortment of tastes. The variety in accommodations and cohesiveness in architectural style along with selection of setting gives evidence of thoughtful planning. The tourist of 1902 might easily have the feeling of being in the wilderness with all the comforts of home at hand.

Within a year LaCoste began to close the pincers on a grandiose scheme to monopolize the Valley's tourist trade. To control the tourist trade required additional land. The largest landowner was the Earl of Dunraven. The Earl had long since left management of his property to the discretion of his American agent, Frank Prestridge, working through the Estes Park Company Ltd. Gaining dominion over the Earl's land would also give LaCoste control of the largest hotel in the area, The Estes Park Hotel.

To purchase the Earl's property required more capital than LaCoste could muster alone. He formed a syndicate known

variously as The Dunraven Syndicate, The Estes Park Syndicate, and The Estes Park Company. In the July 8, 1927 edition
of the Estes Park Trail LaCoste related how he traveled to
England. There, while waiting for weeks to see the Earl, an
agreeable lease was worked out. All that was needed to close
the deal was the Earl's signature. Confident that his dream was
about to come true LaCoste returned to Denver and his job at
the Denver Post.

LaCoste released a grandiose description of the Syndicate's
plans which appeared in the April 3, 1903 edition of The Denver
Republican. The public's appetite for sensationalism along with
exaggeration and embellishment made accuracy the exception
rather than the rule in turn of the century newspapers.
Hyperbole aside, the article gives insight into what LaCoste and
his associates had in mind:

> ...The Estes Park Company... has control of 11,000 acres
> of lands in the park, with 30,000 acres of range lands,
> comprising the former holdings of the Earl of
> Dunraven.... The company is also negotiating for the
> Rustic Hotel with surrounding grounds and Sprague's
> (Lodge)....

The account of the purchase seems to stretch the truth to the
breaking point when it states that "practically all the cottages
in the park not owned by non-residents and kept as their homes
have also been bought by the Syndicate...."

The dry mountain air of Colorado's high country was long
recognized as a treatment for tuberculosis. The Syndicate
wanted to profit from the "camp cure" by building an immense
sanatorium. The Syndicate also planned "to build on the
Dunraven ranch a modern high class summer hotel," because as
they stated, "it has not always been possible to get suitable
accommodations.... With the Park turned into a vast pleasure
ground, and ample provisions for the best food products, all
previous objections will be dissipated."

Recognizing that tourists and summer residents of the Park needed services the Syndicate planned to expand its monopoly in other ways.

> (The Company) will conduct a big general store, and will also provide for the furnishing of nearly all supplies that the park can produce direct to the hotel and cottages. For example, a creamery will be established, so that the best of milk and cream and butter may be obtained. Cattle fattened on the sweet grasses of the hills will be slaughtered, put in cold storage and provided instead of beef brought by wagon from the railroad. All the vegetables which will grow in the mountain valley will be obtained by the hotel keepers....

Knowing that even the best accommodations would stand empty without adequate transportation the article further states that the company "acquired all the stage lines." To facilitate movement within the park the company intended "to build roads to and through all parts of the park, ...to make the park much more accessible...."

Total purchase price was in the neighborhood of $400,000 with improvements estimated at over $100,000. The Syndicate's overall purpose was:

> ...to make the park, not a fashionable resort, but a place where people may go to enjoy the comforts of civilized life, while wearing their old clothes, hunting, fishing, mountaineering or simply loafing.

However, all of these ambitious schemes, whether reality or a giant hoax, were dashed at the hands of the Earl. The Syndicate's plans for 1903 were smashed, however, when the "temperamental Earl had refused to sign the lease and had torn it up in a whimsical tantrum."

In June 1903 another tourist driving a steam powered car bearing his name arrived in Estes Park. Like Dunraven and

LaCoste, he was entranced by the beauty of the Valley. F.O. Stanley quickly became the major player in the attempt to separate the Earl of Dunraven from his land.

Undaunted, LaCoste returned to England in December 1904 to continue his efforts to purchase the Earl's property. There he contacted fellow American, Anna Wolfrom, who was attending Oxford. Surprised to hear from LaCoste whom she had met in Denver, she inquired the nature of his visit. His response was, "to buy Estes Park." He continued, saying that he was representing F.O. Stanley and B.D. Sanborn in the purchase. Anna recalled that they went to the "House of Parliament to deliver some papers to Lord Dunraven." Anna remembered that "in a few minutes a tall man with tufts of reddish hair came out to greet us." Then, after "a word or two from Guy, a bow from Lord Dunraven,... we retraced our steps." Whether he was actually acting as Stanley and Sanborn's agent is not known.

LaCoste succeeded in obtaining a four year lease dated April 21, 1904 with an option to purchase the Earl's Estes Park domain. His lease of the Earl's land is borne out by period advertising listing LaCoste as General Manager of the English Hotel. This was verified in the February 15, 1905 edition of the Ft. Collins Weekly Courier stating that Guy and his brother, Fred, "have rented the English Company's ranch for another year." The exact terms of the 1904 lease aren't known, but records indicate that LaCoste was not able to live up to his end of the bargain since he was $830 in arrears.

A new lease dated June 13, 1905 gave LaCoste and his associates, J.C. Hoover of Hamilton, Ohio; Dr. William S. Bagot of Denver; Albert G. Birch of Washington, D.C.; and Gerald Hughes a seven year lease with option to purchase the Earl's Estes Park domain for the price of $50,000. It must be assumed that LaCoste was the "point" man while the four partners supplied the necessary capital. The rent was $1,850 per year until 1906 when they had to start making improvements to the property amounting to $5,000 per year. Other clauses included the right of LaCoste "to build summer buildings" and to sell plots which would be credited towards the purchase price.

LaCoste had finally accomplished what he had set out to do! He had bought out the Earl and had "control" of Estes Park; however, success for LaCoste was a reluctant mistress. His magnificent scheme all too soon fell apart. Something happened during the ensuing months because on October 5 the county records show LaCoste and The Estes Park Company deeded back "all the property" in Estes Park to the Earl. What happened to cause the deal to collapse? Perhaps the agreement with Stanley and Sanborn, if there was one, soured, or maybe one of the Syndicate's partners had a business reversal.

After 1905 LaCoste dropped from the Estes scene since no more grandiloquent stories appear in the Denver press. He wrote a dime novel entitled Art Thou the Man? published by Dodd, Meade and Company in 1905. In 1907 he sold his interest in the Estes Park Land and Investment Company. LaCoste retained approximately 30 acres encompassing his homestead cabin and some additional acreage for several more years while continuing his newspaper career at the Denver Times and Denver Post.

One wonders what happened to Guy LaCoste's dream. Was the ambitious young man overtaken by the forces which he himself had set in motion, or had he simply bitten off more than he could chew? Soon other speculators including F.O. Stanley and Burton D. Sanborn were able to carve up the Earl's holdings into more manageable pieces.

LaCoste was an incurable optimist and romantic personifying the turn of the century entrepreneurial man. Although LaCoste failed in his magnificent scheme, one imagines that he would approve of the legacy left on his homestead property. The Estes Park Center, YMCA of the Rockies is the largest family resort and conference center in Estes Park and one of the largest in the state of Colorado.

Estes Park as LaCoste knew it.
Courtesy of the Colorado State Historical Society #123   F.P. Clatworthy

Guy LaCoste's dugout and cabin.
Lula W. Dorsey Museum   F.P. Clatworthy

Two outbuildings of the Wind River Lodge.
Lula W. Dorsey Museum   F.P. Clathworthy

The Wind River Lodge.
Lula W. Dorsey Museum   F.P. Clatworthy

Grand Lake Encampment: 1907

The passing years have left the YMCA of the Rockies with a rich and colorful history. The traditional story of the founding of the Western Conference of the YMCA existed in oral tradition for many years. It was related by S.J. Schreiner in his narrative, The Story of the Estes Park Conference, written to commemorate the Association's fiftieth anniversary. The traditional story is rooted in fact, but as with many oral histories, there is a blurring of fact and loss of detail.

The Traditional Story

In his book Sam Schreiner stated:

The story of Estes Park really begins with a mosquito. It all started in Canon City, Colorado, at the 20th Annual Convention of the Colorado State Young Men's Christian Association in February 1907....

As a result, a conference was called to meet at Grand Lake, Colorado, in July of the same year....

Five days were scheduled to discuss their "mutual need for inspiration and training" and on July 13th they resolved to: "...form a property corporation to be known as the Western Conference of the Young Men's Christian Association...."

After designating an executive committee..., the Conference adjourned hastily (two days before the scheduled adjournment) because further deliberations would be unbearable due to a scourge of mosquitoes.

Six of the delegates, including William E. Sweet who had been chosen Chairman of the new Executive Committee, decided to take advantage of the two unexpected days of leisure the mosquitoes gave them to hike over the Continental Divide.

The trail led them north and east. It was a rugged trail that eventually took them over Flat Top Mountain....

The hiking party stopped only a moment to rest after a weary climb to the roof of the world to look with awe and rapture upon this breathtaking vista of mountains and valleys.... The descent was more rapid. The rare atmosphere was already taking on the crisp coldness so characteristic of night in the mountains. The trail was free of snow, and the men hurried as fast as the rare air permitted. Soon they reached timberline and then the view was lost....

When at last Bear Lake was circled, the party dropped quickly into Glacier Valley with its roaring mountain stream splashing its way over boulders and fallen timber, over waterfalls and between high canyon walls. A beautiful paved highway takes the visitor over this rugged mountain area today, but when our hiking party found its way along the stream there was only a foot trail which was not easily visible in the gathering twilight.

Just as the first stars made their appearance in the clear night sky, the hikers had a fleeting glimpse of a light below. In a few moments, they were approaching Wind River Lodge where they found warmth and a friendly welcome.

Morning comes suddenly in this valley as the sun peers cautiously over Sheep Mountain, but the hikers, refreshed after a restful night, were already abroad exploring the setting.... Directly in front of the Lodge were seven pines, tall and stately....

A short walk to the crest of the Mesa revealed the magnificent Mummy Range.... No doubt the snow white glacier wedged into the deep clefts on the face of Ypsilon, forming an unmistakable letter Y, must have suggested that here God had created a place for the YMCA camp and had Himself stamped the... mountain with its insignia.

Before the sextet sat down to a welcome breakfast, they had already, individually, come to a decision. At the table, the conversation quickly revealed the deep impression the scene had made upon them. Shortly, they were in conversation with the owner of Wind River Lodge (Mr. Tucker) to discuss the possibility of holding the first meeting of the Western Conference at Estes Park.

An Historical Account

The YMCA of the Rockies was not created by happenstance. Its origins are immersed in the larger YMCA Movement. Early YMCAs were centered around reading rooms where Bible study and other classes were held. As the programs of the young YMCAs expanded, larger quarters were sought. Libraries, auditoriums, and lecture rooms replaced simple reading rooms. Soon specialized buildings built specifically for Association use replaced rented ones. No longer could the most dedicated layman care for these specialized buildings. That care required a trained professional, the YMCA Secretary.

With the YMCA going through a period of incredible growth in the late nineteenth century, the demand for experienced Association workers always exceeded the supply. During the early 1880s, Associations on the east coast began formal training whereby candidates had a few weeks instruction to gain some practical knowledge of YMCA work.

In 1885 a summer encampment was held at Lake Geneva, Wisconsin. There fifty-seven persons including Secretaries, laymen, and their families gathered for fifteen days in Bible study and discussion of Association work. The idea of summer school encampments for training and study was born. Due to its success, other sections of the country developed similar facilities: Silver Bay, New York; Blue Ridge, North Carolina; Hot Springs, Arkansas; Hollister, Missouri; Lake Forest, Illinois; Arundel-on-the-Bay, Maryland; Asilomar, California; and Seabeck, Washington.

As late as 1895 the YMCA had failed to make inroads into the far western states as there were no Associations in Idaho, Wyoming, Utah, western Colorado, western Texas, or Arizona. Soon after the turn of the century, that state of affairs changed. There were stirrings of the Movement throughout the west. In Colorado, the YMCA entered a period of explosive growth with Associations established in many Front Range cities. The YMCA rode on the shoulders of evangelical fervor into mining camps on both sides of the Continental Divide. While the Movement was being advanced through the efforts of many men of faith, the energy that led to the founding of the YMCA of the Rockies came primarily from two men, William E. Sweet and Bruno Hobbs.

William E. Sweet.
Lula W. Dorsey Museum

William E. Sweet became active in the Denver YMCA shortly after arriving there in 1891 and immediately became one of the most active laymen in the Colorado Movement. In 1901 he was elected President of the Denver Association, a position he held for twenty-five years. Making his financial resources available as well as his time, he pledged $25,000 towards constructing a YMCA building in Denver.

Sweet was also involved "in the desperate... battle... to estab lish YMCAs in most of the larger towns in Colorado." In 1904 he became a member of the International Committee, now the National Council. With characteristic energy he dedicated himself to establishing a permanent encampment in the Rocky Mountain region. As a delegate to the 1907 State YMCA Convention, Sweet may have placed the subject on the agenda.

Sweet was aided greatly by Bruno Hobbs whose involvement with the YMCA began in Kansas where he served as chairman of the State Committee. Moving to Cripple Creek, Colorado in 1899, he entered banking and became active in the YMCA movement. Hobbs began corresponding with the International Committee seeking to hold a regional Student YMCA Conference in Colorado. Through his efforts the first YMCA Student Conference

Bruno Hobbs.
Lula W. Dorsey Museum

was held in Cascade, Colorado in 1908. By the time the encampment was held in Grand Lake, Hobbs was a full time Secretary attached to the International Committee. Joining forces, neither Sweet nor Hobbs would be content until there was a permanent YMCA encampment in the Rocky Mountain region.

The official impetus to organize the Western Conference was put forth at the 20th Annual Convention of the YMCA held at Canon City, Colorado. There the State Executive Committee recommended establishment of a "summer conference and school in the Rocky Mountain District." The idea of annual Association sponsored Bible conferences in Colorado was not a new one. The Association had held annual meetings in Glen Park from 1895 through 1906. Many found that location unsuitable because of the "many resort features and inadequate facilities." The State Committee's recommendation was put to a specially appointed committee comprised of F.L. Starrett, William E.

Sweet, Clarence P. Dodge, Charles B. Hall, and Gus S. Bilheimer. After conferring they issued the following statement:

> That the State Committee plan to hold a mid-summer Bible Conference, to be participated in by all city and student Association men... and that the support of the International Committee be requested in the establishing of a permanent summer conference as soon as possible.

After issuing its statement, the committee made arrangements for a preliminary conference at Grand Lake, July 11 through 16, 1907. Invitations were extended to Association leaders in Colorado, Nebraska, Kansas, Missouri, Texas, Arizona, New Mexico, Utah, and Wyoming.

It was likely the encampment was held west of the Continental Divide to encourage participation by western delegates. It certainly offered a more secluded setting compared to Glen Park. There, the delegates found peace and quiet while contemplating the task at hand. A 1909 YMCA pamphlet gives credibility to that thought stating:

> During the summer of nineteen hundred and seven a group of thirty Association men from half a dozen Western States spent a week in a camp at the side of Grand Lake, Colorado. Here on the shores of this peaceful little body of water, in the shadow of mighty mountain peaks was born the Western Conference of Young Men's Christian Associations. After a week of quiet, earnest prayer, and conference, these men...decided that at some point in the Rocky Mountains of Colorado there should be established a retreat for Association men.

In 1907 Grand Lake had a thriving but highly seasonal economy, neither backward nor primitive. From the beginning, Grand Lake was famous for its fishing as well as picturesque beauty. It was "discovered" early on by wealthy Denverites seeking refuge during the short but hot Denver summers. They followed in the steps of trappers, miners, and hunters. For the most part the new visitors were only tourists, simply camping out or staying in one of the hotels.

Grand Lake as the founders of the Western Conference saw it.
Denver Public Library, Western History Department

Grand Lake had basked in its isolation until 1905 when David Moffat's Denver, Northwestern and Pacific Railroad reached Granby via Rollins Pass. Now Grand Lake was reached in relative ease by stage from Granby, and the community entered into what Patience Kemp called its "golden age." The wealthy bought lake front property and built summer homes. When the YMCA delegates arrived in 1907 Grand Lake had several hotels including the Grand Lake Hotel, Nickelson House, Kaufman House, and Rustic Inn as well as numerous tourist camps.

When the conference convened at Grand Lake, the following Association leaders were in attendance:

F.L. Starrett, William E. Sweet, James H. Causey, Gus S. Bilheimer, M.N. Dillon, Leroy Burdick, and W.F. Tucker of Denver, Colorado; D.E. Dobins of Boulder, Colorado; J.L. Synder of Smuggler, Colorado; Orno E. Tyler, of Ft. Logan, Colorado; J.P. Bailey of Omaha, Nebraska; C.M. Mayne of Lincoln, Nebraska; K.A. Shumaker and George E. Lerrigo of Topeka, Kansas; Rev. Walter C. Veazie of Dallas, Texas; C.G. Titus of El Paso, Texas; C.S. Bishop of Kansas City, Missouri; D.W. Pollard, of Bisbee, Arizona; Rev. Harris H. Gregg, D.D. of St. Louis, Missouri; W.H. Day and Bruno Hobbs, secretaries of the International Committee.

Assisting in the conference were C.H. Douglas, W.C. Burkhart, John Rawlins, Roy Terrell, Dr. John Wethered, and Arthur Bosworth. Although the official records fail to indicate it, there were at least ten women, nine children, and two dogs at the conference. A total of at least 59 individuals can be counted in a group photograph. The Grand Lake Encampment was located at the east of downtown on the present site of the Rapids Hotel. There, a dining tent and seven sleeping tents were pitched in the open field.

On Wednesday evening July 10 the encampment was opened with a devotional by Rev. Veazie as the group gathered around a campfire. Rev. Gregg formally opened the encampment the next morning at 8 o'clock with Bible study. Rev. Veazie conducted a final devotional service each day at 8:45 p.m. Opening the day with Bible study and closing with a devotional was a time honored tradition in YMCA encampments. The pattern was repeated throughout the six days.

On Friday July 12 the conferees moved towards taking care of the business at hand. After the opening Bible study, there ensued a general discussion concerning establishment of a permanent annual summer Bible conference and training school. That was followed by a presentation on the following aspects of the subject:

"The Need," by Bruno Hobbs
"The Field," by C.G. Titus
"The Scope," by Gus Bilheimer

By the next day the conferees were ready to act. Just after the regular morning Bible study a formal plan of organization was submitted and the following motion was made:

> That the active members of Young Men's Christian Associations present at the Conference form a property corporation to be known as the Western Conference of Young Men's Christian Associations, to provide facilities and cooperate in the conduct of conferences, institutes, and other assemblies of Young Men's Christian Association workers; to acquire and control such property as may be necessary for the above purpose; and to request the endorsement and cooperation of the State, Territorial, and International Committees; the Conference to be located in the State of Colorado.

Afterwards a group of twenty-one men were elected to serve on the Board of Directors. William E. Sweet, Clarence P. Dodge, D.E. Dobbins, James H. Causey, and H.H. Tangeman were appointed to prepare and sign Articles of Incorporation.

An election of officers was then held with William E. Sweet elected President, John C. Wharton, O.A. Boyle and James H. Causey as Vice-Presidents, Charles B. Hall as Secretary, and Clarence P. Dodge as Treasurer.

A motion was made to petition the "International Committee to conduct on the grounds of the Western Conference of Young Men's Christian Associations, a regular annual summer conference for student associations, beginning in 1908."

Not all time was spent in work at the Grand Lake encampment. The presence of horses attests to the fact the local environs were explored. At least one side trip was taken to Columbine Lake where armloads of columbine were picked.

One last piece of business was conducted before adjournment. The officers along with G.S. Bilheimer, J.P. Bailey, and K.A. Shumaker were appointed to "select a location for the holding of the Conference of 1908...." With that, the meeting was adjourned.

The official record doesn't mention mosquitoes as did Sam Schreiner's story. Since the founders were camped out on the shores of the largest natural lake in Colorado, the mosquitoes must at times have made life miserable. Years later around the campfire in front of the Administration Building, some remember William E. Sweet recalling the founding of the Association. One of his favorite stories was about the voraciousness of the Grand Lake mosquitoes!

Encampment tents (center left) at the edge of Grand Lake.
Lula W. Dorsey Museum

The Grand Lake Encampment.
Lula W. Dorsey Museum

Delegates and their families.
Lula W. Dorsey Museum

After adjournment the conferees' trail led eastward towards Estes Park. According to E.T. Colton, a biographer of Sweet, the trip eastward had the earmarks of a "personally conducted routing." Estes Park had been a vacation destination for the Sweet family for several years. Sweet was certainly aware of the Wind River Lodge since it had "for several summers been a day's excursion point for the Sweet family." According to Colton the six hikers including Sweet, Bruno Hobbs, Clarence P. Dodge, George E. Lerrigo, C.E. Titus, and Gus S. Bilheimer spent the night at the Wind River Lodge.

Both Colton and Schreiner failed to mention a second group, which traveled to Loveland by train and to Estes by steamer. The groups met in downtown Estes Park where they posed in front of F.P. Clatworthy's "Ye Lyttle Shoppe." The combined groups then toured the Estes Valley in search of suitable sites for the 1908 encampment.

How much consideration was given to holding the 1908 encampment in Grand Lake is not clear. However, it is obvious that there was some. In September 1907 C.P Dodge sent an invitation to the International Committee in New York "from the Grand Lake, Colorado, Association Conference Committee" asking their support in arranging "a Student Conference on the grounds at Grand Lake in 1908." Other than its isolation, it is unclear why Grand Lake was ruled out.

The founders pose in front of F.P. Clatworthy's studio in Estes Park
Lula W. Dorsey Museum   F.P Clatworthy

Research suggests a more logical decision was made to consider Estes Park. A 1909 pamphlet gives credence to that methodical approach by stating:

In accordance... a Committee of men made careful investigation during the year that followed, and selected Estes Park, Colorado, as the place above all others for the location of a permanent summer conference ground.

The process and exact timetable involved in selecting the Wind River Lodge is much more lengthy than the oral story suggests. At a November 23, 1907 meeting of the Western Conference in Washington, D.C., the decision had not yet been made; however, August 1908 was selected as the date for a "Volunteers' Conference."

On December 26 the Executive Committee of the Board met at the Albany Hotel in Denver to continue planning for the August encampment. A budget of $2,500 was adopted and Gus Bilheimer was approved as the Association's first paid employee at a salary of $500 for three months. A formal motion was made to hold the 1908 meeting at Estes Park for ten days between July 15 and August 15. There is evidence supporting the idea that consideration was given to renting the Elkhorn Lodge, Longs Peak Inn, or Horseshoe Inn. Those hotels, however, exhibited the exact resort atmosphere the Committee sought to avoid.

It was not until February 7 that Bilheimer was directed "to negotiate for Wind River Lodge in Estes Park... with power to act." What factors had finally tipped the scales in favor of the Wind River Lodge are lost. The quiet solitude and majestic surroundings certainly played a role, and the letter "Y" outlined in the glaciated face of Mt. Ypsilon assuredly had not gone unnoticed in the selection process. It is very easy to believe that Sweet had it planned that way from the beginning.

All was in readiness for the 1908 Conference....

The First Estes Park Conference 1908

One can imagine the profound anticipation felt by friends of the Western Conference preceding the scheduled July conference. During the spring and early summer, the Conference was widely advertised in publications such as <u>Association Men</u> and the <u>Denver Young Men</u>. There was much behind the scenes work to be done such as renting tents and arranging for transportation. When July finally came and the dream was realized, the sense of fulfillment must have been exhilarating.

"Getting There" in 1908

Getting to Estes Park in 1908 was an adventure, especially for "flat landers" visiting the Rocky Mountains for the first time. Wiley Foster Spencer was among the young YMCA Secretaries attending the first encampment. As a youth, he felt a strong calling to the Methodist ministry. The fact that his father was a Methodist preacher and that he was named after two bishops certainly had something to do with the "call." Spencer became convinced that he could not tolerate the church's autocracy; therefore, he sought and found fulfillment in the Young Men's Christian Association.

Wiley Spencer had recently graduated from the Business School of Baker University and accepted the position of Executive Secretary at the YMCA in Kansas City, Missouri. He had just finished a new home for his bride to be, Ina Belle, on the edge of town. By coming to Estes Park, he would have the opportunity to hear inspirational speakers, meet fellow Association workers and laymen, and gain a wider understanding of the Movement he had chosen as his vocation. Besides, Spencer loved to fish and never missed an opportunity to "wet his line."

Spencer's California Express train pulled out of the Union Pacific station in Kansas City on Thursday July 30 at 10:05 a.m. Ahead lay 640 miles of mostly featureless plain between him and Denver. The afternoon run across the blazing, parched Kansas landscape was miserable as fields shimmered and mirages danced on the horizon. At 7:55 p.m. he arrived in Ellis, Kansas, just as the day's heat was waning. Departing Ellis, he reset his watch to Mountain Standard time. At first light, between Deer Trail and Byers, Spencer caught his first glimpse of the Front Range.

The train pulled into the Denver station at 6:30 a.m. He had plenty of time for breakfast and to stretch cramped muscles before reboarding for the final leg of his trip. The Western Conference secured a special package rate with the Colorado & Southern Lines and the Loveland-Estes Park Automobile Company saving Spencer $2.10 off the regular price of $9.60. The train pulled out of Denver at 8:15 a.m. for a 61 mile journey paralleling the spine of the Rockies. The twin peaks of Longs and Meeker were visible the entire way. Arriving in Loveland at 10:45 a.m. there was just enough time to catch the eleven o'clock stage for the 22 mile trip to Estes Park.

When Wiley Spencer stepped off the train he was greeted by a line of five Stanley Steamers whistling softly like calliopes. Two of them were the large 30 horsepower Model Z Mountain Wagons designed by the Stanley brothers for stage line work. The other three were five passenger cars. The last car was filled with photographic equipment belonging to F.P. Clatworthy. After everyone was ready, they posed for a photograph in front of the station. Their luggage followed later in a steamer baggage wagon.

The caravan headed west out of town with Clatworthy's car going on ahead. The road wound along the Big Thompson River. Suddenly, a gap in the seemingly impenetrable wall of the mountains opened up, and they were in the Narrows of the Big Thompson Canyon. A few hundred yards ahead, Clatworthy's car was parked. They stopped long enough for him to take several photographs from a ledge above the road. The breeze blowing down the canyon was cool, much cooler than the heat of the plains.

The cars creaked and groaned as they made their way up the rough canyon road. After some time the canyon widened. They were at the Halfway House in Drake and stopped only long enough to get a much needed drink and let the drivers fill the tanks of the steamers from the Big Thompson River. Soon they were headed towards Estes again.

Steamers at the Loveland train station.
Lula W. Dorsey Museum

F.P. Clatworthy

Steamers in the Narrows of the Big Thompson Canyon.
Lula W. Dorsey Museum   F.P Clatworthy

The Half Way House at Drake.
Lula W. Dorsey Museum   L.C. McClure

Estes Park, circa 1908.
Lula W. Dorsey Museum   L.C. McClure

When they reached the head of the canyon, a vast green valley stretched out in front of Spencer. With the Valley rimmed by snow capped peaks, he felt as if he were at Heaven's gate. Soon they reached the little village of Estes Park. Not stopping, they passed through town heading westward. Four miles out of town they came to Kibby Corner where they crossed the Big Thompson and ascended the last hill. On the open mesa lay a sea of white tents. They stopped at a big tent under a banner proclaiming "YMCA Headquarters." Wiley Spencer was assigned to tent #15. For ten days he enjoyed fellowship, inspiration, renewal of spirit, and a little fishing.

Wiley Foster Spencer (right) prepares to go fishing.
Lula W. Dorsey Museum

The Encampment

An advertising pamphlet described the 1908 encampment as being "held in a little city of canvas." The tents were arranged in a hollow square pattern surrounding a never dying campfire typical of YMCA encampments. W.O. Fletcher of the Loveland Reporter provided a detailed description:

> Wind River is in a most beautiful location for mountain views... with a most beautiful valley to the southeast, seemingly headed by Long's Peak and looking so near in the bright morning sun that one is almost persuaded he has but a few hours walk to reach its summit.
>
> In this valley the YMCA has tents and assembly grounds. Tents to the number of fifty of 8 X 10 size are arranged around a square of some 200 X 200 feet, with an assembly tent of 26 X 50... and a dining tent... flanked by the cook's cabin. In the center are huge logs for camp fire and good cheer.
>
> Many states were represented.... We noticed delegates from Arizona, Kansas, Missouri, Minnesota, Utah, Nebraska, Oregon, Texas, and Arkansas, with a representative from the little kingdom of Korea.
>
> The services on Sunday morning were most excellent. Rev. H. H. Gregg of St. Louis gave a most impressive discourse upon "Righteousness as God's Gift." Good singing was a feature of the service, emphasized by a mixed quartet, closing with a male duet....
>
> Such gatherings... at such a place for the YMCA give new life to the movement, and those visitors from abroad will carry away a greater reverence for Nature's God and an enthusiasm for their work....
> The assembly closes August 10th.

The Estes Park Mountaineer provided a somewhat shorter but equally insightful description:

The sessions are to close Sunday, with a big meeting here. The monster tent will be brought down from Wind River and erected in the city park, across from the school house. Good speakers are promised, and the occasion should be made much of by the town people.

A sea of tents...
Lula W. Dorsey Museum

Official records indicate 93 delegates attended the conference from July 31 through August 10. Evidently that number, being almost double the capacity of the Lodge, exceeded the expectations of the Western Conference. Consequently, fifty tents were rented to accommodate the crowd. The tents were located in the field in front of the present location of the Lula W. Dorsey Museum across from Raton cabin.

To keep distractions at a minimum the Executive Committee moved that the Conference "be for men only and that accommodation be secured at Sprague's (Lodge) for the families of delegates." By the time promotional literature was issued, plans had changed since it was suggested that accompanying families stay at the Wind River Lodge a scant half mile from the encampment.

A glimpse into the day-to-day pattern of life during the Encampment comes from Association Men:

> At the institutes the morning is given to serious hard study... for thorough training for Association work. The afternoon is given to recreation. Camp fire talks follow the supper hour, then stimulating addresses, entertainments, and musical features. Excursions are run frequently to points of interest.

As the article indicates, not all time was spent in work. The delegates found the mountains and streams enticing. Photographic evidence suggests that at least one trip up Longs Peak was made.

The Mr. Tucker of oral tradition was in charge of the commissary. His experience at the conference was somewhat less than pleasant according to the Mountaineer:

> W.F. Tucker... was kicked in the face by a horse Monday, receiving a bad cut on the lip and a bruised arm. His injuries caused him much pain, but he was able to continue his duties.

Mr. Tucker was also the subject of one of the few entries in the 1908 Board Minutes. He had contracted to feed "75 people for the full time..." and his bill was in dispute.

The 1908 Volunteer Workers Conference was a resounding success. The September issue of Association Men stated that:

> ...(It) was recognized as one of the strongest American conferences, with (a) large place on the program for devotional and inspirational Bible study.... This place

will become a permanent feature with equipment for a series of western Association gatherings, including the Student Conference.

While the first conference was a rousing spiritual success, its finances did not fare as well. Expenses amounted to $1622.55 of which only $190 was offset by fees. The rest had to be made up by pledges and subscriptions. At the end of August the Western Conference had only 45 cents in the bank!

Mrs. Hobbs in front of tent #3.
Lula W. Dorsey Museum

Building a Permanent Home

Throughout the winter of 1908 official records were silent concerning selection of a permanent site for the Western Conference. Finally, on March 16, 1909 Charles B. Hall, Secretary, reported that he had entered into negotiations with the Estes Park Land and Investment Company for purchase of the Wind River Lodge. The purchase price of $8,500 included 334 acres, hotel buildings, and other property.

Getting Things Off the Ground

At the March 9 meeting of the Estes Park Land and Investment Company there was mention of a possible hitch that might prevent the sale from being finalized. The Minutes state that the Company will "use all reasonable effort to acquire a good and merchantable title to the above described lands... prior to January 1, 1910." Guy LaCoste had, like so many homesteaders, only squatted on the land and failed to file for a patent. That was rectified on October 8, 1908 when a homestead patent was issued to "Guy Robert LaCosta." The misspelling of LaCoste's last name set off a new round of legal paperwork as affidavits were filed attesting to the fact that Guy Robert LaCosta was one and the same as Guy Robert LaCoste.

The late spring purchase of the property precluded any improvements for 1909. Mr. A.G. Pearson of Wichita, Kansas was employed as Executive Secretary at $2,100 per annum. Dates for "The Vacation Conference" were set for July 17-25. Pearson was directed to secure two leaders for the conference,

"one a Bible teacher and the other an inspirational speaker."
Rather than two, four leaders were selected including Rev.
Robert Freeman, Rev. Perry V. Jenness, Rev. Howard Agnew
Johnston, and Edward W. Peck. Board and lodging for the
conference was $12. That "scale (applied) to ladies and other
visitors" as well.

The major item of discussion at the July 24, 1909 Board
meeting was financing the major improvements planned for the
Conference grounds. A significant fund raising effort was
initiated during the winter of 1908, and by July 1909, $15,000
of the needed $25,000 was raised.

A.A. Hyde, a successful businessman from Wichita, Kansas
befriended the Western Conference early on. In 1889, he found-
ed the Yucca Company which
grew into the highly successful
Mentholatum Company. Hyde
saw God as his partner in life
and business. Rather than the
normal Christian tithe of 10%, he
often shared 90% of his profits
with over 60 charitable organizations and hundreds of individuals. During the early years of
the Association, Hyde made sub-

A.A. Hyde.
Lula W. Dorsey Museum

stantial contributions and guaranteed numerous notes and also
gave unselfishly of his time and love.

In anticipation of the planned expansion, the Board
authorized the Committee on Buildings and Grounds to employ
a landscape gardener, architect, and engineer and to prepare a
site plan. Two months later the Board authorized the Committee to:

...proceed with a water and sewer system, dining hall, and such buildings and other improvements as will be necessary to get ready for the entertainment of the Student Conference next June at a cost of approximately $15,000.

Thomas P. Barber was authorized to prepare plans for buildings. Before adjourning, the members expanded their motion asking Barber to submit plans and estimates for a dining hall, twenty-five tent cottages, administration building, and auditorium. While contemplating the improvements, the Conference was shocked to learn of the accidental drowning in New York of Bruno Hobbs. A.A. Hyde immediately pledged $2,000 towards construction of a Bruno Hobbs Memorial Auditorium which was unanimously supported by the Board.

The fall of 1909 saw the young Western Conference with too much to do and precious little time to do it. Secretary Pearson, seeking financial support for the new Association, traveled extensively throughout the eastern states armed only with photographs of Estes Park and a dream. By October the reality of the situation had obviously set in. The Board's vision of what it wanted to accomplish before June was far too ambitious, and they began to investigate ways to cut corners.

As a cost cutting measure, six tent cottages and fourteen tents replaced the planned twenty-five tent cottages. The dining hall, administration building and auditorium were combined into a Dining and Social Hall. Fred J. Beckstrom of Boulder was awarded a contract for construction of the Dining and Social Hall at a cost of $8,750.

The architectural style employed in the Dining and Social Hall carried out the Western Stick theme initiated by the Estes Park Land and Investment Company. Where the Lodge used that style in a rustic manner, the Dining and Social Hall represented a formalized interpretation of Western Stick.

Typically, buildings of that style are chalet like in appearance.
The Dining and Social Hall differed from the mainstream by
showing a much rarer Oriental influence. Viewed from the
front, its massive roof seems supported by a central core making
it appear to almost float above its foundation much the same as
temples of the far east. Western Stick was also evidenced by
rustic railings, posts, and lattice work on the gables.

Dining and Social Hall under construction.
Lula W. Dorsey Museum

The Dining and Social Hall's original 1910 interior was very
stark with white plaster walls and square, angular trim.
Whether this was due to a hurried construction schedule or cost
cutting measures is not clear. Lighting for 1910 was by means
of table lamps and brass kerosene lamps hung from the ceiling.
The kitchen was in the area now occupied by the administrative
offices just behind the present front desk. Furnishings included
rocking chairs, long tables, and area rugs.

The Board decided to move the main buildings of the Wind
River Lodge from their original location to the central part of
the campus. Four buildings were relocated. The moving of the

Wind River Lodge from the side of Bible Point to the corner of Kallenberg and Rainbow Drives must have caused quite a stir. Although no photographic documentation exists, an interesting story of its relocation was passed down by Mrs. Gussie Freeburg. Her husband, M.M., was on Fred Beckstrom's crew moving the Lodge. According to her, the Lodge was moved on log rollers placed one in front of the other. The teamster in charge of the horses was inexperienced and almost lost the Lodge when the team got out of control.

Three other buildings including "the seven room cottage," a "three room cottage," and a one room log cabin were relocated as well. The larger cabin, (Mariposa), was moved to the site presently occupied by Alpen Inn where it remained until torn down circa 1933. The three room cabin, (Purple Finch), was moved to a spot just east of Hyde Memorial Chapel where it still sits. Purple Finch served as the administrative office until 1911 or 1912 when suitable space became available. The one room cabin was placed behind the relocated Wind River Lodge.

As spring turned into summer, construction delays forced the scheduled Student Conference to be moved to Cascade, Colorado. The June 16 Loveland Reporter stated that the grounds showed "lots of work accomplished as well as a great deal yet to do." The roof of the Dining and Social Hall was shingled, but the interior was unfinished. "A force of twenty men (were) working hard to have it in shape for the three hundred guests expected on July 8th." It's highly probable that the water and sewer systems were likewise unfinished. However, by early July the grounds were sufficiently ready to accommodate the 125 delegates attending the Vacation Conference from Friday, July 8 through Sunday, July 17.

Success had come at a high price. The Association's total liabilities amounted to $41,800. On the positive side, income from the single conference combined with rental income from the six tent cottages and Lodge had paid for all operating expenses incurred during the summer.

Tho Dining and Sooial Hall 1910.
Lula W. Dorsey Museum

The kitchen in the Dining and Social Hall 1910.
Lula W. Dorsey Museum

Relocated Lodge, Dining and Social Hall, and Tent Cottages in 1910.
Lula W. Dorsey Museum

The Hyde family relaxes in front of a tent cabin.
Hyde Family Album courtesy of John Hyde

The Golden Years

The vision of the founding fathers of the Western Conference was rewarded by success beyond their greatest expectations. The young organization had the "Midas touch" turning everything to gold. The Summer School was a rousing success gaining recognition throughout the YMCA Movement. Building after building was constructed to keep pace with the demands of a growing Summer School. The YMCA adjusted to changing clientele by accommodating conferences outside of the Summer School umbrella and building housekeeping cabins for families. It was a time of experimentation. It was also a time of social change as women began to make their presence felt at the male dominated YMCA.

The Western Association School

The motivating force behind the founding of the Western Conference was the Summer School. As such, almost every aspect of the Association's affairs was dictated by the needs of the School during the early years. The Association realized that a formal structure was needed for its training program if it was to attract students and instructors from throughout the YMCA Movement. In 1911 the Western Association School was formally organized "in a systematic way for employed officers" which included graded class work. The nine institutes included Boys' Work, Railroad Work, Laymen, Younger Secretaries, Older Secretaries, County Work, Physical Work, Pastors, and Secretarial Wives.

Summer Schools
DAILY SCHEDULE

July 27th to August 9th, Inclusive

Hour	Subject	Instructor

7:00 BREAKFAST

8:00 to 8:45 Introduction to Bible Study............................Mr. Hopkins
Life and Works of Jesus.................................Mr. Paige
Christ's Teachings for Boy Workers.......................Mr. Hall
Old Testament History....................................Mr. Lute
Personal Evangelism ....Mr. Puehler
Early Days of the Christian Church.....................Mr. Scott
Biblical Pedagogy ....Dr. Honline

INTERMISSION

8:55 to 9:40 Business Management (City)............................Mr. Manley
Boys' Work for General Secretaries......................Mr. Flynn
Membership Methods and Social Work....................Mr. Scott
Restaurant Management—Elementary—First Half.....Mr. Benning
Restaurant Management—Advanced—Second Half......Mr. Benning
Religious Work in Railroad Communities—Second Half..Mr. Coulter
Secretarial Relations—First Half.......................Mr. Knebel
Church History—First Half.............................Mr. Nichols
Railroad Transportation—Second Half....................Mr. Adams
Religious Work in Industrial Communities—First Half.Mr. Hopkins
Coming Americans—Second Half........................Mr. Rindge
Administration of the Physical Department...............Mr. Wetz
First Aid ....Mr. Reisner
Physical Examinations ....Dr. Kallenberg
Laboratory Methods ....Dr. Newhall
Methods of Country Work ....Mr. Pierce
The Development of Leaders.............................Mr. Wood
Rural Church Work ....Dr. ....
Animal Husbandry ....Mr. Morton
Methods and Principles of Boys' Work...................Mr. Cotton
Layworkers' Round Table ....Mr. Shuey

INTERMISSION

9:50 to 10:35 Association History ....Mr. Coulter
Religious Work, Principles and Methods...................Mr. Lute
Educational Work, Principles and Methods..............Mr. Nichols
City Seminar...Mr. Wood
Principles and Organization of Railroad Work.......Mr. Richardson
Business Management (Railroad) ....Mr. Day
Railroad Seminar.............Messrs. Knebel, Richardson, Minear
The Association in Industry ....Mr. Rindge
Mass Athletics ....Mr. Kearns
Construction and Equipment ....Dr. Kallenberg

Summer Schools
DAILY SCHEDULE

July 27th to August 9th, Inclusive

Hour	Subject	Instructor

9:50 to 10:35
Non-Equipment Physical Activities ....Mr. Erps
Methods of Country Work—Advanced..................Mr. Hatfield
Country Seminar ....Mr. Roberts
Agronomy ....Mr. Jardine
Methods and Principles of Boys' Work...................Mr. Cotton
Methods and Principles of Boys' Work—Advanced.........Mr. Hall
Boys' Seminar ....Mr. Ritchie
Boys' Seminar—Advanced ....Mr. Flynn

INTERMISSION

10:45 to 11:30
Personal Life of the Secretary (City)....................Mr. Paige
Association Building—Its Care and Upkeep.................Mr. Day
Relations and Power of the Association in the Community.Mr. Wood
Applied Psychology .... Dr. Honline
Personal Life of the Secretary (Railroad)—First Half...Mr. Knebel
Housekeeping—Second Half ....Mr. Minear
Social Work—First Half ....Mr. Minear
Educational Work—Second Half.......................Mr. Benning
Anatomy ....Dr. Newhall
Physiology ....Mr. Wetz
Hygiene ....Mr. Erps
Principles of Country Work...........................Mr. Hatfield
Principles of Country Work—Advanced ....Mr. Roberts
Program for Church Workers with Boys.................Mr. Flynn
Program for High School Workers with Boys............Mr. Cotton
Community Work for Boys ....Mr. Ritchie

INTERMISSION

11:40 to 12:25 Platform Hour..Dr. Stone

12:30 DINNER

1:30 to 2:15
Gymnasium Practice—Elementary ....Mr. Kearns
Gymnasium Practice—Advanced ....Mr. Schmidt
Pastors' Seminar ....Dr. ....
2:30 to 3:15 Calisthenics—Advanced ....Mr. Schmidt

6:00 SUPPER

7:00 to 8:00 GAMES FOR EVERYONE

8:00 to 9:30 STUDY PERIOD

10:00 LIGHTS OUT

The 1912 Vacation Conference, as the School was called, included 75 students, 17 faculty, and 52 other guests. Students paid a registration fee of $1 and $4 for tuition. Room and board was $22 for the 14 3/4 day period. In 1913, enrollment increased to 110. For the first time college aged Student Secretaries were recognized as part of the School program. As an added bonus to the Association, Summer School students brought over 100 family members and guests with them.

As the name Vacation Conference implied, not all the time was spent in study. Afternoons were left open for recreation. Sports such as volleyball, baseball, and tennis were played in the field in front of the Administration Building. The surrounding natural splendor offered its own entertainment in the form of fishing, horseback riding and hiking. From the first year, Longs Peak beckoned, and lakes like shining jewels summoned the adventurous. Evenings were reserved for special events such as the Campfire Program begun in 1911. Sundays were kept in the best Protestant tradition. "All amusement features and unnecessary labor (were) omitted on (that) day." Sunday offered another chance to hear the intellectual giants of the day.

Hikers on their way up Longs Peak.
Lula W. Dorsey Museum

As the reputation of the Western Conference spread, it quickly outgrew the regionality reflected in its name. Students from around the world were attracted to Estes Park. In 1912, the name of the Western Conference was changed to the Estes Park Conference of the Young Men's Christian Association.

By 1914 the summer school bulletin began to take on the appearance of a college catalog with class times, course descriptions, and instructors listed. The standard course of study consisted of 12 days of classes with one-half day for examinations. A typical day at the Western Association School included five class periods. First period was reserved for Bible Study which was required for every student. Technical courses were scheduled for periods two through four. The last period of the day was reserved for Platform Hour which highlighted some of the most respected speakers of the day sharing views on contemporary issues. Platform speakers included Dr. John Timothy Stone, A.A. Hyde, John R. Mott, William Allen White, and Billy Sunday.

The Summer School attracted leaders from throughout the YMCA Movement to Estes Park to teach and head the various departments comprising the Western Association School. Dean of the Physical School, Henry F. Kallenberg, epitomized the wealth of knowledge and talent to which students were exposed. Kallenberg was a man of "firsts" in the physical education field. He was the "first physical director in a student YMCA-YWCA," "first paid football coach at the University of Iowa," "first to develop the idea of a water gymnasium," and "first to introduce mass athletics."

Henry Kallenberg grew up in New York City, learning to swim in the Hudson River. A devotee of physical activity, he entered into every form of athletic competition available to him. During his teens he and a companion rowed around Manhattan Island.

Kallenberg taught at the YMCA International Training School in Springfield, Massachusetts for two years beginning in 1889. Among his students were Amos Alonzo Stagg (famous football coach) and James Naismith (inventor of basketball). Later Naismith sent Kallenberg a copy of the rules of the new game asking him to try it at the University of Iowa. Kallenberg made two quick changes including cutting the teams to five per side from the original nine and putting a small hole in the bottom of the peach basket so that the ball was retrieved by poking a stick up through the opening.

After earning a medical degree he served as the Director of the Department of Hygiene and Physical Education at the Secretarial Institute and Training School of the YMCA (George Williams University). In that capacity Kallenberg was responsible for developing a graded summer school program with a sequence of prescribed courses.

In 1915 the Summer School Dean, Gus Bilheimer, reported that enrollment had increased by 15%, and four large tents were rented for use as classrooms to accommodate the increase. This was especially heartening to Estes Park supporters when all other Association schools had shown declines. The Summer School Committee further stated that:

Students in the Summer School have brought more of their families and guests with them this year than at any time in our history. We find that men are coming to Estes Park from outside our recognized territory more and more every year, drawn by the strong program as well as by natural attractions.

Enrollment increased dramatically in 1917 and 1918 when a special War Work School was organized to train Association workers for service "Over There." In 1917 Bilheimer reported that 83 of the school's 203 students were attending the special School. The War Work School required special course work including thirty minutes of military calisthenics in the morning and evening lectures designed to prepare Association workers for the rigors of life on the front line. Before war's end, nearly half of the YMCA Secretaries were lost to enlistment and War Work requiring emergency readjustment on the home front.

C. Howard Hopkins recounted the magnitude of the War Work effort between 1917-21. Over 26,000 Association workers including 3,480 women expended $152,000,000. YMCA War Work was not limited to serving service men overseas. Stateside, 952 buildings were hastily erected to serve soldiers in training camps. Over 1,500 YMCA Secretaries accompanied 1,102 troop ship sailings. In England 1,025,000 American troops were served in 155 locations. In France 1,944,300 soldiers were ministered to in wooden huts, tents, and rented facilities requiring the services of 885 workers.

One of those to serve in the War Work effort was Henry Kallenberg. Arriving in Germany after the Armistice, he rendered invaluable service. His job was to boost the Army of Occupation's morale through physical activity. Kallenberg was asked to train a group of American soldiers for a demonstration in mass athletics for the Inter-Allied Games held at Pershing Stadium in Paris. He returned to the United States in July after completing his tour of duty for the YMCA.

Service to Allied soldiers came at a price that could not be measured in dollars. According to Hopkins 286 YMCA workers died of disease, were killed in action, or died of other causes. Association workers received 319 citations including Order of the British Empire, French Legion d' Honneur, Distinguished Service Cross, and Distinguished Service Medal.

In spite of increased enrollment from the War Work School and the overall success of the School, expenses continued to exceed income. Money collected from hotel operations was not sufficient to pay both the operating expenses and cover the Summer School shortfall. Various means were attempted to ease the burden on the Association. Assessments were levied on State YMCA Committees sending students. Appeals were also made to the International Committee and to Estes Park Conference supporters. The financial support received was minimal, and continuing deficits plagued the Summer School throughout its existence.

Morning calisthenics at the War Work School, 1917.
Lula W. Dorsey Museum

Army YMCA in Waco, Texas.
Lula W. Dorsey Museum

Henry Kallenberg (center, second row with mustache) and his students.
Lula W. Dorsey Museum

Faculty, students, and guests of the Association School.
Lula W. Dorsey Museum

The first Summer School graduates.
Lula W. Dorsey Museum

The first Christmas in July celebration, 1912.
Lula W. Dorsey Museum

The Association Branches Out

While the Conference was established as a training school, it was only logical that others outside the Summer School would want access to the grounds. In 1910 the Board took its first step by stating:

> ...that the officers of the Conference be authorized to grant the use of the Conference grounds and property at such times and under such conditions and terms, and to such parties or organizations as may be in keeping with the purpose of (the YMCA).

It was reasoned that these groups could benefit from the inspirational setting and the many fine instructors in residence as a result of the Summer School. Besides, new conferences would bring much needed income to offset Summer School deficits and provide funds for expansion. The first group to hold meetings on the grounds not under direct control of the Summer School was the YMCA Student Conference in 1912. In 1913 it was followed by the Rocky Mountain YMCA Student Conference, YMCA National Student Secretary Conference, City YWCA Conference, and Student YWCA Conference. These groups, along with the Summer School, filled accommodations from June 10 to September 1. While they obviously fell under the umbrella of the YMCA Movement, their use of the grounds marked a milestone in the development of the YMCA of the Rockies.

In 1914 a Pandora's box was opened when Chi Omega Fraternity (Sorority) inquired about holding its national convention in Estes Park. The staunchly conservative Board of Directors was shaken to its soul by the proposition. After a lively discussion concerning the possible detrimental affect the group might have on the atmosphere of the Association, the Board gave conditional approval when it:

> RESOLVED, that the tentative action of the Executive Secretary in considering favorably the request of the Chi Omega Fraternity (Sorority) for entertainment for their National Convention in 1914, which action was taken upon the advice of several directors, be approved,.... however, that... should not be a precedent for... entertainment of non-religious bodies, and that no such action be taken henceforth without the consent of the Executive Committee or the Board of Directors, and be it further RESOLVED, that the contract with the Chi Omega Fraternity shall carefully provide for the maintenance of all standards of the Estes Park Conference..., especially for Sabbath observance....

Whether it was the Board's conservative stance or other considerations, Chi Omega eventually declined to hold its meeting on the grounds. The positive or negative result, depending on one's position, was that next time the decision was easier.

Early in 1917 A.A. Hyde recommended that the Association investigate the possibility of conducting a Laymen's Conference for five days under direction of the Summer School. Pastors were urged "to come with leading laymen from their churches." The Christian Workers Conference was held during the middle ten days of July for pastors and laymen. It almost proved disastrous when instructors canceled, but A.A. Hyde and J.H. Causey quickly stepped in for the absent leaders.

The delegates were so inspired by the conference that Hyde obtained pledges from 40 pastors to come the next year and bring someone with them. In spite of the apparent success, the YMCA lost $700 on the proposition. On the positive side, the Rural Pastors Institute was born, which proved one of the more successful early non-YMCA groups using the grounds.

The Board and management quickly found that catering to conference groups was a risky business. In 1917 the YWCA decided to hold its meetings in the east, leaving a large number of vacant beds. Management was authorized to negotiate with the Rocky Mountain Osteopathic Association for use of the grounds. Again the conservative Board issued a resolution reminding management the action was "undertaken as an experiment and applies to 1917 business only, and shall not be considered a permanent policy...."

During the next several years the range of groups served continued to expand including the Interchurch World Movement, YWCA High School Girls Conference, Missionary Education Movement, YWCA Community Conference, Ex-Service Mens' Conference, Epworth League Institute, Baptist Young Peoples Union, and Zeta Tau Alpha Fraternity.

Kansas City YWCA City Conference, 1913.
Lula W. Dorsey Museum

Conference groups outside of the Summer School were not the only ones wanting access to the grounds. At the annual Board meeting in August 1914 "the question of summer cottages for house-keeping purposes to be rented to Association men" was brought up. That subject had far reaching implications for the Association's future. Until that time all accommodations were strictly for sleeping purposes. Summer School and conference delegates and their families ate in the Dining Hall. As the name implied, housekeeping cottages would have a kitchens for cooking.

Sleeping cottages were divided into two types. The original tent cottages consisted of a wooden floor, frame, and shingle roof. The outside walls were made of heavy canvas. The "door" was a simple canvas flap that was propped up awning style to serve as a porch. Inside, canvas partitions divided cottages into four bedrooms. The sleeping tents were even simpler affairs consisting of wooden floors, wooden half walls and frame roof covered with canvas. Equipment included two beds and bedding, two folding chairs, bedside stand, oil lamp, washbowl and pitcher, and slop jar.

By 1914 tent cottages took on a more permanent appearance with canvas walls being replaced by half wood and half canvas, while doors replaced canvas flaps. The sleeping tents were relegated to employee housing. Both types were typical of YMCA encampments and tourist accommodations in Estes Park where people expected to "rough it."

A special committee was appointed to study how other summer Associations handled this matter and to report at the next annual meeting. While the committee was compiling its report, Bilheimer was authorized to accept an advance of $1,000 from A.A. Hyde to build and equip three housekeeping cottages on an experimental basis. When the committee reported in August 1916 it stated, "the situation is a complicated one needing many safeguards...." Mr. Bilheimer was obviously looking at the dollar side of the balance sheet when he stated, "our experience with these furnished cottages this year leads me to believe that it would be desirable for us to increase the number." Citing the fact that he could have rented a score or more, he asked the Conference to build nine to twelve more cottages. He saw an added benefit in that the tenants would provide beneficial advertising. In spite of his obvious optimism Bilheimer did show some misgivings on the subject:

> I would also suggest that the directors consider seriously the effect on the work of the School and the Conference of a large number of women and children who will always be resident in these furnished cottages While there are many advantages, there are some distinct drawbacks, and the whole problem should be carefully considered.

Before adjourning, the Board approved building six additional cottages. John Timothy Stone offered funds to build five small cottages at $1,000 each. These cabins were to be held for use by "Sunday-School Missionaries, Ministers, and YMCA Secretaries." Stone's offer was quickly accepted by the Board, but some off the record lobbying by Board members resulted in Dr. Stone withdrawing his offer, because it might interfere "with the School spirit."

In 1919 it was reported that there were an "unusual number" of cabin inquiries despite rates being raised to $150 for the summer. For that year 11 housekeeping cottages were rented for the entire season and 6 for substantial periods. The upward spiral in demand for cottages and use of the grounds by individuals outside the auspices of the Summer School was only a prelude to the coming decades.

Early housekeeping cabin.
Lula W. Dorsey Museum

Success Brings a Building Boom

The early success of the Summer School quickly brought
about the realization that many more improvements to the
grounds were necessary. A.A. Hyde secured the services of a
landscape architect who submitted a master plan including roads
and locations of buildings. The Board accepted the plan and
authorized the Executive Committee to spend $5,000 or what-
ever necessary to provide "such additional sleeping, dining hall,
sanitary and recreative accommodations and facilities as may be
necessary."

To finance the expansion required an enormous infusion of
capital. John D. Rockefeller was approached to contribute
$40,000. Through lengthy negotiations, Rockefeller's share was
set at $15,000 with the Conference raising $35,000. Thus, the

Conference would have its improvements and be debt free by September 1, 1913. Since the Board had already contracted to accommodate a conference of 200 in 1911 immediate action was required. On January 1, 1911, the Western Conference sold bonds totaling $17,000 due December 31, 1913. Executive Secretary Gus Bilheimer was authorized to spend $2,000 to bring the capacity of the grounds up to 200.

In February 1911 a bid for $2,750 was submitted by Fred J. Beckstrom for the construction of a gymnasium. It was a hasty substitute for the $20,000 Bruno Hobbs Memorial Auditorium proposed by A.A. Hyde in 1909. This building was the core of the present Walnut Room serving as the first Assembly Hall in 1911 and 1912.

Placing their faith in God that gifts to complete the fund raising campaign were forthcoming, the Board authorized numerous improvements to the grounds during the winter of 1912-13. In July, A.A. Hyde reported that $30,000 had been expended. He continued:

> ...we have planned for and let contracts and supervised construction of the following improvements: Assembly Hall (Hyde Memorial), addition to and remodeling Dining Hall (Walnut Room), twenty tent cottages, garage (Maintenance), laundry, water and sewage systems.

When the Gymnasium was remodeled into the Dining Hall, the old kitchen in the Dining and Social Hall (Administration Building) was remodeled into bathrooms. In July, as the deadline for Rockefeller's gift came due, the Conference found itself $9,000 short in raising its share. Three Board members stepped forth to guarantee the amount. Clarence P. Dodge pledged $5,000, A.A. Hyde $3,000, and William E. Sweet $1,000.

Adequate classroom space for the Summer School was a recognized problem from the first years. Dissatisfied with the four large tents housing classes, Gus Bilheimer requested funds to build permanent classrooms in 1915. Funds became available when $1,000 was donated by participating state Associations to build five suitable buildings. Two were kept lighted at night for a study hall and another served as a night time employee recreation hall.

Growth of the Summer School demanded continued improvements to the Conference property. In 1917 the Business and Property Committee presented a list of items it deemed essential. These included electric lights, bath house, additional classroom space, additional sleeping cottages, outdoor swimming pool, golf course, six additional tennis courts, and a large auditorium. Studies were undertaken to assess the feasibility of the proposed improvements.

Action on electric lights was deferred as was the golf course. It was also decided the existing tennis courts were sufficient. Mr. Sweet took care of the auditorium situation by donating $1,000 to increase the seating capacity of the Assembly Hall by fifty percent.

The matter of additional classroom space was solved by the time tested practice of bartering when the Conference offered its worn out Stanley Steamer to Ruel Anderson in exchange for building a classroom. Mr. Hyde had purchased a new Model T truck for the Conference in 1914, and for over a year Executive Secretary Dillon had tried without success to dispose of the steamer. Mr. Anderson obviously got more trouble from the steamer than he bargained for and refused to finish the job. The Board directed Dillon to settle the dispute in what ever manner seemed fair to get rid of the troublesome beast. With completion of this classroom, the original six "state" buildings: Texas, Oklahoma, Nebraska, Arkansas, Kansas, and Colorado were completed.

The grounds, circa 1913.
Lula W. Dorsey Museum

The new "state" classrooms.
Lula W. Dorsey Museum

The YMCA Goes Into the Real Estate Business

When the Association initially purchased 334 acres in 1909 there seemed to be more land than could ever be developed. When fund raising for improvements to the grounds fell short, it was suggested that the Association plat and sell lots as a method of raising funds. After much discussion the sale of property was approved.

Initially, extensive private ownership within the grounds was planned including numerous sites around the northeast side of the circle across from the present tennis courts. Lots were priced from $200 to $1,000. Promotional literature stressed the Christian atmosphere of the YMCA as well as the natural beauty of Estes Park. Mr. Hyde was given the honor of choosing the first lot. Selecting one near the entrance to the Conference grounds he built his summer home, Lower Hyde, in 1910.

The ambitious plan for selling lots was quickly down-scaled after concerns were expressed over future property needs of the Association. Consequently, future private lot sales were concentrated in the Overlook Subdivision south of the main grounds and near the original site of the Wind River Lodge. There was also concern as to whom lots would be sold. In August 1916 the Committee on Building Sites "was instructed to sell building sites only to Christian men who would be in thorough sympathy with the purposes of the Conference...." Deeds on the property protected the Association with restrictions including a prohibition on making or consumption of alcohol, keeping the Sabbath, and allowing the YMCA first right of refusal to repurchase the property when it came up for sale.

Mr. Hyde was soon followed by others, many of whom already had ties to the YMCA. Some of those families continued to take an active role in the affairs of the Association for decades.

A.A. Hyde's private cabin.
Lula W. Dorsey Museum

A Snow Storm of Epic Proportions

In 1913 Estes Park was struck by a legendary snowstorm as recounted in the Estes Park Trail Gazette:

Early December gave every indication of a storm in the making. Stock was restless; the air was heavy, causing unrest even among the men who were working for us.

In the morning snow started falling from a very quiet and heavy-laden sky. The snow fell hour after hour with unremitting beauty. Hardly any wind moved, and then when it did, it came in very, very gently from the north-northeast.

This continued... steadily for two days and nights and then ceased for two days, leaving approximately three feet of snow on the level. The usual wind did not develop, and then the snow began again in the same quiet beautiful pattern, hour after hour.

And when the sky cleared in two, or a little more, days, there were a few inches over six feet of snow.

It started snowing in Denver on Monday December 1. Forty-five and one-half inches of heavy, wet snow fell on top of eight inches already on the ground. Transportation and communications ground to a halt. Hotels filled with stranded workers and travelers. This was not an isolated storm. It snowed from Wyoming to New Mexico and from Leadville to Greeley.

Damage was widespread throughout the Estes Valley. The town was completely cut off from the outside world. Supplies and food were in short supply. At the YMCA of the Rockies, the recently remodeled Dining Hall collapsed under the load. The Administration Building and several cabins were damaged as well. In the spring broken dishes and other debris were loaded into wagons and hauled to a site just above the present YMCA stable and dumped. Even today, pieces of broken glass, turned purple by the sun, can be found lying on top of the ground. Damage was quickly repaired in time for the 1914 season.

The collapsed Dining Hall, spring 1913.
Lula W. Dorsey Museum

Downtown Estes Park after the big snow.
Courtesy of the Estes Park Area Historical Museum

Cows, Hogs, Potatoes, and Ice

During the early years, the Board and management eagerly looked for ways to save money. The most creative one was farming. With the last frost in late May and the first one in early September, farming at 8000 ft. is risky at best. Add in poor soil, droughts, hail, deer, and rodents and the odds of failure increase.

Not to be deterred by the odds, Executive Secretary Gus Bilheimer suggested in August 1914:

That we employ a practical farmer early in the spring next year and make a vigorous effort to grow all of our own garden produce, hay, etc., and that we also purchase a sufficient number of cows to operate our own dairy. I believe that this will save money and give us a much better product than we now have. Our experience in a small way with a truck garden this season demonstrated, I think, our ability to grow necessary garden produce on a larger scale.

Bilheimer continued the farming experiment in 1915, reporting that the vegetable garden was expanded "growing considerably more" than last year. He began experimenting with potatoes and indicated that in "another year we could grow all the potatoes we need for our own consumption, and more if desired." Bilheimer was also convinced that the YMCA:

> ...could raise all the hay we need and thus save the two hundred or two hundred and fifty dollars we are now expending for hay, and probably could raise some oats.

Before ending his report, Bilheimer had one final suggestion, namely, starting a hog farm. He stated that the garbage was presently being hauled off "by a neighboring hog grower, who is feeding between forty and fifty hogs, satisfactorily, from our refuse. The profit in these might be ours...."

The Board authorized Bilheimer to continue expanding the farming project. Lee Miller was employed and given responsibility for farming operations. This decision was influenced by Bilheimer's announcement that "we secured about seven thousand pounds of potatoes" in 1915 saving the conference $140. His 1916 report showed mixed results:

> Because of the dry season our garden has not done so well. We purchased forty pigs at a total cost of approximately $175.00 and these have taken care of all our garbage. They have already grown to double their weight.... (We) ought to realize at least one hundred dollars on this investment... besides providing a satisfactory way of disposing of our garbage.

Besides raising a few vegetables, the YMCA raised the ire of Dr. J. A. Weaver of Greeley who purchased a lot from the YMCA in 1916. The potato farm was relocated to the open field bounded by the present stable, Coleman Lane, and the Jellison Youth Building which just happened to front his property. When Mr. and Mrs. Weaver arrived the next year to decide on the placement of the garage they were moved to write a letter to the Board. In part, they stated, "our disappointment was very great when we found the beautiful slope of grass in front of the lot had... been put into potatoes." The Association quickly repurchased the property.

Not willing to be left out of the great farming experiment, A.A. Hyde loaned $1,000 to the YMCA to purchase a dairy herd and equipment. The first five cows did not prove satisfactory; therefore, Hyde asked the assistance of the Colorado Agricultural College in selecting seven good cows. The cows had to be wintered in Lyons and brought up to Estes Park in the summer. Executive Director Ira Lute indicated the lack of success with the dairy herd in his 1918 report to the Board:

> Only four of our cows became fresh this spring and our milk supply has been only about thirty-four quarts a day. Most of this has been consumed by our cottagers, milk for the dining-room is being purchased from the Estes Park Creamery Company. We have kept the cows on pasture awaiting your decision as to the future.

It was determined that a herd of 12 cows and one bull was not large enough to be practical. In February 1919 the Board reached a consensus to discontinue the dairy herd.

Farming on the grounds continued on a fairly large scale until at least 1921 when camp farmer Lee Miller returned to Missouri. Overall results from the farm experiment were marginal. In some years the potato crop amounted to 1000 bushels, and in other years it was a total failure. The same went for vegetables, oats, and hay. Hog farming was mentioned only once which might have had something to do with the odor associated with pig raising. Income from farming was last listed on the annual audit in 1928.

The most successful of the "farming" endeavors was cutting ice. Purchasing ice for the Dining Hall and a growing number of housekeeping cabins was expensive for the Association; so, it was an obvious area for cost cutting. On Wind River, just upstream from the present Dorsey Lake, a shallow depression was flooded during the winter. The exact year ice was first harvested is unclear, but very quickly the YMCA found that it could cut more ice than was needed for the short summer season. Surplus ice was sold to nearby resorts providing much needed income. As the Association's demand for ice increased, commercial cutting was ceased. Wind River supplied ice for domestic use by the YMCA until the early 1950s.

Ed Parton cuts ice on Wind River.
Parton family album courtesy of Beverly Parton Bowen

Trouble With Neighbors

While the Conference was growing so was the popularity of the newly created Rocky Mountain National Park. The original entrance to the Park was one-half mile below the current entrance to the grounds near the present Park Lodge. Then known as Kibby Corner, it was a bustling intersection where the road branched north into Moraine Park and south to the Conference Grounds. From the YMCA the road went over the saddle between Emerald Mountain and Bible Point and into Bartholf Park (Glacier Basin). Thus all the traffic going to Bear Lake was funneled through the center of the YMCA. It was no wonder that in August 1917 it was noted that "the travel through our grounds and in front of our buildings of people going to Bartholf Park has become... annoying...." The Board ordered management to work with the Estes Park Improvement Association to get a new road to Bartholf Park via Glacier Creek. The Board offered $100 for survey work to get the project underway. Work was completed by 1918 as it was reported "practically all of the traffic through our grounds to the Bartholf Park section" has been eliminated.

Problems with the new Park manifested themselves in other ways as well. In 1915, Executive Secretary Gus Bilheimer was notified that the Park would no longer allow the YMCA to cut firewood. Bilheimer complained that this would force the Association to burn expensive coal, so the Board mounted a campaign to get the decision reversed. The proximity of the grounds to the new Park brought incursions of unwanted campers. In 1917 the 126 acres between Glacier Creek and the YMCA property were being leased to a man for use as a campground. These "transient campers" were seen as a threat to the atmosphere of the Association. As a result, the Board purchased 60 acres in late 1917. The remaining acreage was bought by Hyde and Sweet and held until the YMCA had sufficient funds to acquire it.

In August 1918 Dr. Stone related concerns of some local
hotel owners. They expressed distress over what they considered
low rates the Association was charging its guests. They viewed
it as unfair competition. The Board referred the matter to the
Executive Committee for study. Secretary Lute managed to
smooth ruffled feathers by joining the Estes Park Improvement
Association and Estes Park Hotel Association. The Board also
invited local businessmen including photographer F.P. Clatworthy and grocer Fay Brainard to serve on the Board.

Kibby Corner, site of present Park Lodge and Dunraven Inn.
Courtesy of Rocky Mountain National Park Archives

The First Fire

On July 1, 1916 the YMCA suffered its first fire when the
laundry, boiler and engine room were entirely destroyed.
According to Bilheimer:

The fire originated by ignition of gasoline caused by the
cleaning of a skirt. To the splendid service of our

employees and guests and the fact that our water system stood the unusual test... we owe the saving of our dining hall and probably other buildings.

A comical story has come down through the years concerning this fire. When the alarm was sounded, employees and guests responded grabbing anything that held water. A.A. Hyde reacted likewise and was spotted running across the field carrying his slop bucket! The laundry was sorely needed and although totally destroyed, it was rebuilt and back in operation in nine days to meet the midsummer demand.

Bible Point

Other than Mt. Ypsilon, probably no other geological feature is more closely tied to the YMCA of the Rockies than Bible Point. Although shorter and more accessible than surrounding vantage points, it offers outstanding views of the YMCA, Glacier Basin, and surrounding environs. In the time of Guy LaCoste, it was known as Buena Vista. The name was changed as a result of the tragic death of Edwin Bradt whose grave is at the summit of Bible Point. The marker reads:

Born October 3, 1899
Died June 12, 1918
"A normal life"

Although only reaching the age of eighteen, Edwin Bradt's life was anything but normal when compared to most young men of his time. At the age of 12, he traveled around the world for a year with his family visiting missionaries and world-renowned places.

In 1914 he made his first visit to Estes Park. An adventure-some soul, he reveled in the natural beauty. He climbed several mountains, including Longs Peak. Returning to Estes Park in 1916, Edwin attended the YMCA Student Conference with his father, Gordon. After the conference, they stayed to build a cabin on land given to the family by A.A. Hyde. The work was exceedingly hard. Even water for cement had to be hauled up from the YMCA to the building site just below Buena Vista.

Edwin Bradt in happier times.
Courtesy of Bradt family.

In June 1918 Edwin Bradt and a college friend started from Chicago to Seattle to attend the wedding of Bradt's brother. In Nebraska, Edwin Bradt was killed in an automobile accident. At his father's request, the body was taken to Estes Park where the funeral was held in the Assembly Hall (Hyde Memorial Chapel). Dr. John Timothy Stone conducted the services. Employees of the YMCA carried the casket to the base of a big boulder above the Bradt cottage at Buena Vista where Bradt was buried.

Beside the grave the Bradt family placed a mailbox containing a Bible and register for hikers. Over the years, the old name gradually faded away to be replaced with Bible Point.

Ira Lute Oversees a Major Expansion

In February 1918 the Denver Association was asked to share its Executive Director, Ira Lute, with the Estes Park Conference. Besides his devotion to the YMCA movement, Lute was an astute businessman possessing a keen analytical mind. He led the Conference for the next ten years. In 1921 Lute expressed his philosophy of operating the Association:

> Just as a person's mind and spirit cannot reach the highest development and make the largest contribution to success in an imperfect body, (I feel) that the objec-

tives of the Estes Park Conference (are) not capable of
their fullest attainment without adequate mechanical
equipment and an effective smoothly-running organization.

When Lute assumed his duties he quickly set about putting
that philosophy in action by analyzing the business and administrative side of the Association. He divided duties into departments including Administration, Business, Property, and Hotel.
To staff those departments he sought professionals. From the
Denver YMCA, he secured L.L. Radford and Ella Waterhouse for
the Business Department. He turned to the St. Louis YMCA for
the services of M.T. Baird to head up the Property Department.
These people like Lute were only part time employees of the
Estes Park Conference serving in a shared capacity with their
home Associations.

Lute showed concern about the short duration of time that
the grounds were in use each summer as illustrated by his 1918
annual report:

About the middle of June several of us in executive
positions came on the grounds with a limited amount of
help and were followed on July first by the kitchen and
dining room employees, tent maids, bell boys, etc....

Everything was put in "running order" for the Missionary
Education Movement Conference on July 12. He realized that
the overhead involved in such a short season was eating up any
profits, leading to increased deficits and borrowing. He stated
that some necessary work was not being done "owing to
financial stringency and our indebtedness."

By the annual Board meeting in August 1918 concern over
indebtedness and lack of money for improvements began to
weigh heavily on the Board. Therefore, they resolved:

> That it is essential that this property be freed from debt
> and that imperative improvements be made thereon so
> that it may be ready for the largest measure of service
> as a Christian Training Center....

An ambitious goal of $50,000 was set, along with an equally ambitious completion date of September 1, 1919. To kick off the campaign, Dr. Stone pledged to raise $10,000. In December 1918, William E. Sweet, Gus Bilheimer, and Ira Lute traveled to Atlantic City by train. The long train ride from Denver to Omaha gave them time to consider the many needs of the Conference. Stopping in Omaha they met with Dr. Stone. Together they telegraphed A.A. Hyde in Wichita and made a joint decision to raise the goal. The $100,000 Debt and Improvement Fund was to be completed by September 1920.

This was to be a grand fund raising campaign with William E. Sweet as chairperson and Lute serving as secretary. Board members were asked to seek contributions in their respective spheres of influence. State Associations in the Western Region were given quotas. Dr. Stone visited with John D. Rockefeller who pledged $10,000. The deadline was again extended to December 31, 1921. Even while the Debt and Improvement Campaign was being conducted, the Board voted to borrow $25,000 for essential improvements. While this was viewed as rash by some, for the Board it was simply an act of faith.

A major project completed during the campaign was electrification of the grounds. While the official records do not make much of the enterprise, the three Executive Secretaries lobbying over a seven year period must have been delighted when it was announced "light fixtures are being hung" in April 1919. F.O. Stanley brought electric lighting to the village of Estes Park when he opened the Stanley Hotel in 1909; however, it was slow to spread through the Valley. When the YMCA bought the Wind River Lodge in 1909, twenty-five "lamps and chimneys" and eight "candlesticks" were listed on the inventory. Oil lamps, kerosene lanterns, and campfires provided light during the first two summer conferences.

When the Dining and Social Hall was completed in 1910, large brass kerosene lanterns suspended from the ceiling provided light for evening gatherings. Since W.C. Coleman of the Coleman company was among the early supporters of the YMCA, it was only natural to turn to him for assistance. Short on cash but with plenty of property, the YMCA offered to trade Mr. Coleman land in exchange for a gas lighting system. By 1912 gasoline fixtures fueled from central tanks replaced kerosene lighting in the main buildings.

The first mention of bringing electricity to the grounds occurred in February of 1912 when a "wish list" was prepared for John D. Rockefeller. It came up a second time in January of 1914 when Executive Secretary Gus Bilheimer requested the Board of Directors take up the issue. His request was flatly denied due to cost. Undaunted, Bilheimer made another attempt in August 1915 when he reported:

> Our gasoline lighting system in the main buildings, and kerosene in the tents, is far from satisfactory and is costing us for labor and supplies approximately three to four hundred dollars per season.

As if to whet their appetites for electric lights he continued by stating that "lines are now within two hundred yards of our grounds..." at Kibby Corner (Park Lodge - Dunraven Inn). Their attention caught, the Board instructed "the Committee on Business... to investigate and report at the next annual meeting, on the matter of the cost of installation... of electric lights."

The question of electric lighting was shelved being buried in committee or omitted in the haste of improving the property. Finally, in August 1917 the Business and Property Committee recommended a number of improvements including electric lights.

However, the Board again deferred electric lighting in 1918. Lute was left to make the existing gas system work for another year. Making the best of it, he enlisted the help of Mr. Coleman who "came up early from Wichita and at considerable expense of time and of money..., put our lighting equipment in first-class working condition for the season." By the next year Lute joined his predecessors in calling for electricity. He reported to the Board, "We can (no) longer get along with our present lighting system. It is worn out."

Rather than connecting to the existing power network, Lute suggested that a ten horsepower generator be purchased which could be powered by the existing steam engine. As another cost cutting measure Lute suggested that only the main buildings and classrooms be electrified. This avoided "complications of electric irons, electric curlers, electric water heaters, and breakage...." In 1919 the Board finally gave its approval authorizing $1,500 for the project with completion by summer.

The Conference generated it own electricity until 1927 when it connected with Stanley Light and Power Company. The old generating system was left intact for back-up purposes.

On December 31, 1921 the Debt and Improvement Campaign was completed with Dr. Stone picking up all delinquent pledges. When pledges and cash on hand were totaled the $100,000 goal was surpassed by over $3,000! The Board proudly announced that "all improvements were paid for and all indebtedness was paid off, mortgages canceled, and releases obtained."

While the Campaign was in progress the Association began making improvements as money was contributed. When staff arrived on the Conference grounds in 1920, they were greeted with new housing. Previously, staff was relegated to living in disintegrating tents, cast off as tent cottages were built for guests. The behavior of unsupervised female staff concerned their supervising matrons and management alike. Consequently, new staff housing was hurriedly constructed. Fern-Odessa and Pioneer Lodge as they are known today were considered "deluxe" staff housing with steam heat and shower houses.

Improvements continued in 1921. At the front entrance a new stone bridge with rock pillars spanned Wind River. Windows in the classroom buildings were changed from canvas to glass.

The most notable change was the new grocery store and post office building. The original commissary was operated out of a large tent, located where Sweet Memorial Building sits today. With the advent of housekeeping cottages, the commissary was moved to the kitchen causing much confusion. The Association Camp Post Office, which commenced operations in 1916, was housed in the overcrowded Administration Building. The logical solution was to construct a building to house both.

For several years Dining Hall operations were a point of discussion. Waiters brandishing enormous trays served each table individually in a highly inefficient manner. The cafeteria style method of serving was just coming into vogue. After several years of agitation, management was allowed to employ this type of service from a remodeled kitchen.

After lengthy debates the Board allowed camping on the grounds 1921. Located east of the potato patch on the northwest corner of the grounds, the initial plan was to equip the site with running water, toilets, and a caretaker's building. On review of the situation, the improvements were kept to necessary minimums. Consequently only a dozen or so families made use of the Association's first campground.

During the following two years Board and management pored over previous "wish lists" adding, deleting and combining projects. In 1922 a relatively minor expenditure of $1,500 was allotted to replace the aging stable located on Glacier Creek. The new barn was situated in the draw between the main campus and the Second Mesa.

In 1923 the Conference constructed its first truly modern cabins. The "Japanese Indians": Ohshiko, Nakayagi, Moosquin, Wisawanik, Anekus, and Tonashi were located on the Second Mesa on Indian Trail. Advertising literature listed these cabins as Class A, stating:

> While of the same general construction as other cottages they are larger and more completely equipped. They have a living room, two bed rooms, kitchen and bath room. The cottages rest on a cement foundation and are equipped with electric lights. Because of the extra bed room and the well equipped bath room and toilet, these cottages are listed highest in the scale of prices.

Rates for the season were $250. Monthly rates varied from $75 to $135 and weekly rates from $30 to $45 depending on the month.

In 1924 the Association embarked on a spending spree of over $60,000. The Administration Building received a major addition with completion of a bath house. Long identified as a needed facility, it provided a service for guests whose tent cabins lacked showers. Initially, the Conference planned to build both a bath house and a swimming pool. In the planning stages since 1910, the pool was forever being pushed down the list of priorities. In 1913 it was placed on the list for the $50,000 campaign, but after necessary improvements were made, no money was left. The pool came closer to reality when New York architect Louis E. Jallade was commissioned to draw plans for a combination swimming pool and bath house. When the estimated $10,000 cost was presented to the Board all plans for the pool were dropped, and what was left was a simple bath house.

The other major addition to facilities was enlargement of the Wind River Lodge. Hotel income had long been a financial bright spot. Consequently, there was much discussion about building a new modern lodge. Economic reality forced the Board to make do with an addition. The addition almost tripled the size of the Lodge. It consisted of a center section with the bottom floor containing a lobby and the second floor providing sleeping rooms. The west end provided additional accommodations as well as shower facilities and bathrooms. The west end was an exact duplicate in size of the original Lodge. The new building, symmetrically shaped like a barbell bent in the middle, graced the corner of Kallenberg and Rainbow drives for the next 55 years.

Several less significant projects rounded out the 1924 building spree. The 1919 electrical system had already reached capacity. So, the system was upgraded and the entire grounds wired for electric lights. In the Administration Building a new vault was built. A new "Machinery Hall" was added to the existing laundry to house the new boiler, dynamo, and power tools. A sundial with mountain locator was placed in the field in front of the Administration Building.

Proposed bathhouse and swimming pool addition.
Lula W. Dorsey Museum

The bathhouse after cutting costs.
Lula W. Dorsey Museum

The grounds after the building boom.
Lula W. Dorsey Museum

F. P Clatworthy

Women Make Their Presence Felt

While the Board was busy raising funds for its Debt and Improvement Fund, the Conference's female constituency was flexing its muscles. Women and children, considered a distraction to the Summer School of 1908, grew to a sizable group by the early 1920s when their number almost matched that of men enrolled in classes. The beginnings of programming for wives of YMCA Secretaries can be traced back to the 1911 Secretarial Wives School. By 1920 classes included Bible Study, Child Training, The Relationship of the Wife of an Employed Officer to His Work, The Will of God for a Man's Life, and The Message of Christianity for the New Day.

With meeting space at a premium, women were relegated to a crowded corner in the Administration Building. There was much difficultly in hearing instructors due to the noise from offices, as well as the comings and goings of guests. The women took it upon themselves to provide a building they could call their own. One thing is certain. "Allowing" women to take part in a more formal way in the affairs of the Conference was not solely the result of a liberalization of attitudes on the Board's part. With Summer School attendance beginning to slump, bolstering women and children's programming would provide much needed income from room and board.

The women began raising funds in 1921 for the Women's Building. The Board was all too happy to let the women raise funds even if some of it did come from their pockets! The women raised all but $1,000 of the funds needed. Finished in time for the 1924 season, the Women's Building was described as having "a large attractive stone fireplace, a grand piano, rustic furniture, heads and skins of wild animals and Indian rugs...."

At the close of the 1925 season the women formally organized themselves into the Women's Auxiliary with Mrs. A.

Bruce Minear as President. She was followed by Elizabeth
Carse leading the group for several years. The objective of the
Auxiliary was:

> ...to promote and contribute to the social, spiritual and
> inspirational life of the women of the Conference Camp
> (and) to make it attractive and worthwhile for women
> to accompany employed officers to the Summer School.

While the group was formally structured by necessity it was a
loose association since there was no tuition. Class attendance
was not mandatory. The women increased the draw of the
Auxiliary by making membership open to other women guests
and friends of the Conference.

It was natural for the Women's Building and Auxiliary to
become the focal point for child care and programming. "Junior
Training" and "Kindergarten" are both listed in the 1924
Minutes as activities sponsored by the women. The next year
saw a more formalized structure for youth when an "Older Boys
Club" for boys 17 years and older was sponsored by the Boy's
Work School. By 1926 children were being openly welcomed by
the Conference when one publication stated, "bring them along...
nothing can possibly be finer for the children than two weeks in
the mountains...." However, there were limits. The publication
continued, "children are not expected nor permitted to run wild."
In closing it was suggested that there was a "well-organized
department" for younger children under the direction of Mrs.
C.D. Wolfe.

The children's program quickly outgrew the confines of the
Women's Building and propositions were put forth that there
should be a building especially for children. In 1928 that topic
received a boost when Mr. Hiram Strong of Wichita donated
$500 for Kindernook building which was completed the next
year.

Kindernook, 1929.
Lula W. Dorsey Museum

F. P Clatworthy

While most women were making their presence felt in "traditional" ways, there were others such as the Pifer girls, Anne and Isabel, who made their presence known in less conventional ways. As a YMCA Secretary, their father was involved in the Summer School Program. Beginning in 1920, the family called Iris cabin home using it year after year.

The adventurous teenagers loved hiking and soon became unofficial hikemasters of the YMCA. Some of the ladies with more traditional views of a woman's role just shook their heads saying, "What are those Pifer girls up to now?" Their hiking style imitated that of Enos Mills in which destination and speed were not priorities. Enjoyment of nature was the primary objective. One of their favorite activities was to have hikers sit perfectly still listening to the subtle sounds of nature around them.

Anne Pifer Austill, 1922.
Lula W. Dorsey Museum

For four seasons the sisters guided hikes. Several times each summer they led groups up Longs Peak. Starting from the YMCA at three or four in the morning, they hiked up the Wind River Trail to Highway 7 and on to Longs Peak Inn. Passing the Inn as the sun began to rise, they were greeted by Enos Mills. To control the pace of the hike and help with stragglers, one girl took the lead with the other bringing up the rear. When the trail steepened they sang to keep everyone in step.

On the return trip down the Wind River Trail, the hiking party stopped at the Wigwam Tea Room owned by Anna Wolfrom Dove, friend of Guy LaCoste. Finally, at dark the hikers dragged into the YMCA grounds after hiking 26 miles while gaining and losing 6,200 feet in elevation. They made their way to the Administration Building where they soaked in the deep bathtubs of the bathhouse. The only pay the Pifer girls ever received was a meal purchased by thankful fellow hikers.

In the Spirit of Fellowship

During the expansion and growth of the early 1920s, a grand experiment stands out as a testimony to one man's faith and love for his fellow man. For several years the Conference wanted to fulfill a manifest destiny plan by purchasing a 78 acre tract lying on the north side of the grounds. Acquisition would provide the YMCA with the natural boundaries of Glacier Creek, the Big Thompson River, and Wind River. In 1921, A.A. Hyde purchased the tract from F.O. Stanley for $5,000 and then deeded it to the Conference.

Rather than just handing over land to the Association, Hyde had a plan for the property. He felt that the Conference should have "a place where Christian workers with small income could find accommodations at little or moderate cost and have the advantages of the vacational and inspirational features of the Conference." Hyde had a great vision of what Fellowship Park would embody. In the spirit of the early Christian communities, this was to be a place where "people of all faiths and from all parts of the country" had the opportunity of developing the true spirit of "fellowship and understanding by living together in mutual helpfulness and cooperation."

Hyde took special interest in making this Christian communal living experience a success. Arriving in early June 1922, he personally supervised the layout of Fellowship Park.

He first selected a spot for the Community House near a large glacial boulder, later named "Rock of Ages" by Mrs. F. Todd of Chicago. As the hub of the community, Fellowship House had a large living room, two bathrooms with showers, kitchen with laundry facilities, and manager's quarters.

Surrounding Fellowship House, Hyde located campsites and selected locations for six three room sleeping cabins: Onyx, Agate, Granite, Crystal, Quartz and Mica. He selected long time friend Mrs. Elizabeth Dean Fickett of Ft. Collins, Colorado to manage Fellowship Park. She provided careful oversight of the Fellowship community for over a decade. By June 23 two cabins were ready. Rev. and Mrs. Baxter had the honor of being the first occupants of Fellowship. Some 13 years earlier they were the first to arrive at the 1908 encampment. Through hard work the rest of Fellowship was completed by July 30 for the dedication.

Fellowship Community House, 1922.
Lula W. Dorsey Museum

From 1922 through 1934 meticulous photographic and written records were compiled by B.V. Edworthy. Four large scrapbooks detailed the comings and goings of families and groups. At the end of each season Mrs. Elizabeth Fickett carefully put away the scrapbooks till the next year. They gave newcomers a better understanding of the "spirit of fellowship" and let returning guests reminisce.

Hyde showed infinite wisdom in providing Fellowship only with the necessities and then backing off to allow the community to evolve and develop its own personality. At the time Fellowship was dedicated 73 persons were in residence. Many of them rented space for the season thus forming a nucleus of the community. A committee composed of Mr. B.V. Edworthy, Mrs. Zimmerman and Mr. King formulated a code of ethics governing the Christian community. The governing principal of Fellowship Park stated that "each able-bodied man... will be expected to give... ONE HOUR'S LABOR each day in cutting wood, cleaning up brush, and other work in the true SPIRIT OF FELLOWSHIP and for COMMUNITY BETTERMENT." Other rules were simple. In part they asked persons to use only approved camp sites, build fires in designated spots, not to harass birds or animals, not to pick flowers, to conserve water, and clean up after themselves showing respect for the environment and fellow campers. Hyde's only request was that there be a prayer meeting in Fellowship House at 9 o'clock each evening.

Women were expected to give time to communal cooking, cleaning, making curtains and washing clothes. However, Mrs. Baxter proved hard physical labor was not the sole providence of men when she "pioneered in exhibiting the fellowship spirit and herself cleared sage" brush. A partial list of the work in 1922 included:

1. Baxters - Clearing of sage brush and trimming trees.
2. King - Aspen screen made for rest room.
3. Shepherd - Clearing of sage brush.
4. Giddings - Parchesi board made.

5. Stitt - Graded off sewer ditch and around cesspool.
6. Notestine - Wood chopping, always watched the wood box.
7. Wekesser - Made bulletin board and toilet room fittings.
8. Means - Made wood box for kitchen and camp furniture.

During 1922 over 300 people used Fellowship Park. In the ensuing years, a strong sense of community was developed out of hard work and Christian fellowship.

The concept of the Fellowship Park was widely acclaimed. In 1923 a group of ministers attending the Pastors Fellowship School signed a letter of thanks, saying in part:

We believe that the Conference could do no finer work than to enlarge upon this idea. By bringing to the Conference pastors and their families where they are brought in to close association with YMCA workers there is brought about a better spirit of co-operation and understanding and thus the two organizations can better go on in the work of the Kingdom.

Every one was welcome at Fellowship without hesitancy. A "colored delegation" from Friends and Wichita University camped out in Fellowship. Edworthy recorded that "they were real Fellowship lovers and received full Fellowship treatment from other campers near." Their love of the setting was such that one of them left a poem in the Fellowship scrapbook.

Dr. T. Z. Koo, National YMCA Secretary of China, stayed at Fellowship with his wife and four children while attending a YMCA Employed Officers Conference. Dr. Koo was a dynamic speaker bringing inspiration to guests. He was accompanied by Mr. Wong of Peking, China. Together, they were welcomed into the community and honored by a special dinner and reception.

Over the years Fellowship Park was rented by groups such as YMCA boys' groups, Girl Scouts, and Boy Scouts. However, it was the families returning on a yearly basis that gave Fellowship Park its sense of community.

A High Water Mark

The building boom of 1924 marked an apex for the young Estes Park Conference. From a dream proposed at Canon City and nurtured on the shores of Grand Lake, an amazing feat was accomplished by the Association in 17 years. Unfortunately, the Midas touch was soon to be lost. A series of circumstances, most beyond control of the Association, came together during the next few years that nearly spelled the demise of the Association. The Golden Age of the Estes Park Conference had come to a close.

Camping out in Fellowship Park.
Lula W. Dorsey Museum

Fight for Survival

After 1924 it was apparent that the affairs of the Estes Park Conference were coming unraveled. No single problem in itself was life threatening; however, in concert they proved a formidable opponent. Despair and anguish replaced euphoria of previous years. While the official records of the Association present a bleak view, there were bright spots as guests and staff continued to enjoy the beauty of Estes Park. Many years would pass before the Association emerged into the light of renewed vitality.

The Summer School Falters

In the early 1920s the scope of the School was widened with expansion of the old Railroad Work School into an Industrial and Railroad Work School and formation of a Foremen's School. In spite of the added classifications, enrollment dropped to 168 in 1921 from 285 the previous year, and the deficit climbed to $2,750. Executive Secretary Ira Lute quickly recognized the effect escalating deficits were having on Conference operations. As a consequence, he suggested the formal separation of the Summer School from the Conference. Obviously, Lute realized the implications of what he had proposed when he stated:

> (The) wisdom of this course has been questioned by many who believe that the YMCA Summer School is the heart and soul of the Estes Park Conference and that the Conference would greatly suffer by the separation.

A waning Summer School, 1925.
Lula W. Dorsey Museum

In 1923, deficits continued to escalate with almost $4,000 needed to cover the shortfall. In 1925 the Summer School was described as the "smallest in years" not exceeding 168. Consequently, the deficit rose to $6,000. Ira Lute continued his warnings by stating that, "this matter should be one of serious concern to the Board of Directors." The severity of the problem was readily apparent when it was pointed out that of 80 Western Region Associations listed in the YMCA Year Book, 44 were not represented at the Summer School.

At the request of the Association, Rev. Charles F. Wishart of the Committee on Association Vocation made a thorough study of the Summer School. His main criticism was that the School:

> ...needs to definitely broaden its educational and cultural standing..., courses were largely practical with tendency toward economy..., teachers were weak..., and there were too many teachers from the region.

On the positive side he saw Estes Park as having a good physical plant and beautiful surroundings.

The Board heeded Rev. Wishart's criticisms and spent $2,000 improving its Summer School Program for 1926. Dr. Deerin Call, Secretary of the American Peace Society, was employed to deliver six lectures on "Our Çountry and World Peace," William K. Wright of Dartmouth College taught a two week course on the Philosophy of Religion, and C.W. VanPatten put together a music program. Other improvements included employment of experts in Pedagogy (teaching) and Sociology. The recreational aspects of the School were upgraded by employing outstanding inspirational entertainment such as the Fisk Jubilee Singers. For the first time a concentrated effort was made at interpretation of the scenic beauty to conference delegates, students, and other guests.

Some of the Summer School's problems originated from within the YMCA Movement. As the YMCA grew in complexity, the International Committee which provided organization on the national level became an autocratic bureaucracy. State Committees and local Associations saw the whole organization as unresponsive to their needs. The effect on the Estes Park Conference was a lack of coordinated guidance and financial support. An Association-wide movement began pressing for eradication of the autocracy.

The culmination of democratization within the YMCA Movement came at a Constitutional Convention convened in Cleveland in 1923. There, a federal plan of organization was forged with a democratically elected National Council replacing the International Committee. Under this system, yearly National Council meetings conducted business on behalf of local Associations.

A major provision of the reorganization realigned the states representing the Western Region and moved the regional headquarters from Denver to St. Louis. An always alert Ira Lute attempted to call attention to possible problems in 1924 when he stated:

> The Estes Park Summer Schools are in a critical
> period not because of internal conditions although there
> may be weaknesses.... but because of the possible
> exigencies growing out of the reorganization of our
> work under the plan of the new Constitution.... The
> Board of Directors may well be alert to the effect upon
> this school of a rearrangement of our regional plan of
> organization....

The proximity of Denver to Estes Park had previously made
Association leaders readily available. That support was now
lost.

The relocation placed two important Association summer
schools in the same region, Southwestern at Hollister, Missouri
and Western Association School at Estes Park. With attendance
falling at Hollister, its Board offered to open a dialogue to pool:

> ...our interests in the matter of financial support... (and)
> co-ordinating our programs in such a way that certain
> schools will be emphasized at Hollister and others at
> Estes Park.

Rather than discuss merger or joint operations the Estes
Park Board appointed a committee to study operations of its
school. In July 1926 Ira Lute, several General Secretaries, State
Secretaries, and laymen met to discuss School administration,
finances, and attendance. They arrived at several recom-
mendations including separating operating and school budgets,
launching a fund raising campaign, publicizing the advantages
of the Estes Park School, reducing faculty size, and promoting
attendance by employed officers and Boards of Directors of other
Associations.

In July 1928 the Board realized the futility of going it alone
and accepted Hollister's offer. In February 1929 the Joint
Committee of Ten released its findings. In part it stated that
the cost of maintaining two schools was excessive, many local
Associations did not reimburse their Secretaries for school, the

educational level of many Secretaries exceeded the level of the summer school program, and the general trend was to consolidate and centralize forces for training. From these findings the committee recommended development of a comprehensive educational policy for the Western Region and consolidation of the two schools by 1930. The school would be regionally controlled rather than by either the Estes Park or Hollister Board.

Unfortunately, the merger coincided with the onset of the Depression yielding disappointing results. In Executive Secretary Louis A. Black's annual report, he indicated that only 105 students were enrolled in classes, down 20 from the previous year. The utilization of facilities was down to 50% of capacity. He emphatically stated that unless attendance was increased it was "only a question of a short time before the Conference Grounds will have to be permanently closed." Black continued his dismal review saying:

> It seems to me that this separation of the Summer School from the Estes Park Conference removes the only basis by which the YMCA can be used in connection with the Estes Park Conference and that consideration should be given to changing the name by omitting the YMCA.

It would have been easy for the School to fold. Against the odds, the Board decided to find a way to keep it alive. Moving to build upon the educational foundation of the Conference, negotiations were undertaken with the Iliff School of Theology to cooperatively sponsor the Estes Park School of Religion. For unrecorded reasons this proposition never progressed past the discussion stages.

In a last ditch effort, the Conference turned to the University of Colorado. Dr. Elmore Petersen, Dean of the Extension Division was hired to form an alliance with other universities to hold adult education classes on the grounds under the auspices of the University Extension Center. The Board gave its approval with the condition "that the operation of such courses shall be in harmony with the purpose of the Estes Park Conference of the YMCA." Unfortunately, Dr. Petersen was hired by Harvard before the Extension Center was put into operation. Hastily, a replacement was hired. Mrs. Elizabeth Quereau of the Extension Division of the University of Colorado arranged for extension courses on "vital and popular subjects." She arranged "for several entertainments or concerts each week during the months of July and August...." The undertaking was only marginally successful.

While management scrambled to fill empty beds, the United YMCA Summer Schools of the Western Region was in the midst of total collapse. When attendance in 1931 dropped to 35 students all departments were merged into one Secretarial School. The next year was no better. In 1933, with only nine full time students enrolled, the faculty was asked to pay their own expenses. Consequently, the School was operated only on an informal basis. With discontinuance of the Summer School, the Association hit a spiritual low.

Conferences Follow the Summer School's Lead

Accommodation of non-YMCA conferences continued to be an area of concern. In 1924 Secretary Lute informed the Board that he was hearing comments regarding "use of the grounds by other organizations...." He further suggested that "it may be well for you to formulate a policy for the future."

Some groups such as the Boy Scouts posed no problems in the eyes of the Association. In September 1924 the Conference hosted its first "off season" group. With 781 men attending, the Third Biennial Conference of Boy Scout Executives was the largest group to use the grounds as of that time. As well as the usual YMCA and YWCA affiliated groups, several new groups used the grounds for the first time in the 1920s. They included the Baptist Young People's Union, Supreme Forest Woodmen Circle, and Reformed Presbyterian Young People's Conference.

    Like the YMCA Summer School, conference group numbers started to falter long before the onset of the Depression. In 1926 with the prospects for conference business dismal, Secretary Black indicated that he wanted a policy requiring groups to guarantee a minimum number. This would allow him to contact other groups to maximize use of facilities.

    During the height of the Depression, some of the traditional YMCA, YWCA, and religious conference groups canceled. Those that continued to use the grounds declined in number of delegates. In 1930 Secretary Black stated, "we must not give up without putting forth every effort possible to secure additional groups of a religious, educational, or altruistic nature to hold their conferences here." For the first time, the Conference was forced to consider marketing to fill empty beds. Two years later Secretary Ebersole took the first marketing trip in the history of the Conference, going "back east" in search of business.

Great Western Sugar Company group, 1923.
Lula W. Dorsey Museum   F.P. Clatworthy

Ebersole's efforts went for naught, and the conference business bottomed out when only six groups were scheduled in 1933. With cutbacks in services necessitated by the Depression at its height, several changes were made in conference services. The Pastors' Fellowship School and YMCA Student Secretary's conferences were changed to self programming since there were no instructors from the Western Association School. The 220 person Student Secretary conference was accommodated in housekeeping cabins where they cooked their own meals paying $6.50 for ten days. Unfortunately, the $1,430 collected from the group was largely offset by the loss of Pine cabin which burned at the hands of a group from Kansas.

Changes in Clientele

The decade of the 1920s saw a decided change in the type of tourist visiting Estes Park. The growing love affair between America and its automobiles was partly at fault. Previously, people arrived by train at their vacation destination staying for the duration. The automobile and the mobility it provided encouraged visiting more places. This change in vacation habits was noted by Ira Lute in 1924 when he reported:

> ...a decided change is noticed in the demand for housekeeping cottages. Instead of being rented for the full season in advance, the tendency now seems to be toward shorter terms of from one week to one month.

Shorter stays were encouraged by railroads and travel bureaus offering special packages where several western national parks were visited in a short time.

The question of accommodating "transient" business to fill empty beds was first discussed in 1917 raising the ire of some conservative members of the Board. As the Depression deepened, business in any form was welcome. Executive Secretary Louis Black reported that he had worked out an agreement with Roe Emery, President of the Rocky Mountain Transportation Company, to fill empty beds. This arrangement was credited with saving the 1931 season. Transient, secular business came with a price since there were "several unpleasant occurrences" in the form of late night drinking parties which were strictly against the rules. Seeing a possible way out of a desperate position, the Board allowed Secretary Black to contract for travel groups the next season. Unfortunately, the liberalization of policy came too late because in August 1932 only 29 travel group tourists were accommodated as compared to 330 the previous year.

As tourists' habits changed, their taste in accommodations changed as well. No longer did rustic cottages with canvas windows, outhouses and running water by the door appeal to them. In 1924 a proposal was made to convert all cabins from canvas windows to glass at a cost of $2,100. However, it wasn't until 1928 that the first cabins, Heather, Arbutus, Bittersweet, Laurel and Barberry were given glass windows. As an added bonus the cabins received flush toilets!

The strong demand for cabins prompted one of the few improvements made during hard times. In 1932 canvas partitions were replaced with celotex ones in 15 of the circle cabins in response to negative comments from tourists brought in by travel agencies. With collapse of the agencies, the Board regretted the unneeded expenditure stating, "had we known what we know now regarding the excursion business for the summer, we probably would not have incurred this expense...."

Iris cabin with its new glass windows.
Lula W. Dorsey Museum

Tonashi provided a higher class cabin for guests of the 1930s.
Lula W. Dorsey Museum

A Tale of Woe

The Depression was several years into the future when the Conference began experiencing financial difficulties. To blame the problems of the Estes Park Conference on reorganization of the YMCA, failure of the Summer School, or even the Depression would be simplistic. Some of the problems were self inflicted such as an untimely purchase of land from Dr. John Timothy Stone in 1923. The two parcels totaling 200 acres included The Cliffs, on the eastern edge of the Conference, and The Heights, on the western edge. Stone, liquidating all his Estes Park holdings in preparation for a world tour, offered the property for $30,000 including numerous improvements valued at $63,000. With the Conference out of debt from the Debt and Improvement Campaign, the offer was too tempting to pass up.

All too quickly, the purchase proved unwise. In 1924, The Cliffs property remained unrented "though it was extensively advertised...." The Heights proved equally unrewarding. In a last effort to salvage something of the season, The Heights was operated on the American plan at $17.50 per week with Bungalow cabin serving as a dining hall. The next year proved disappointing as well for The Cliffs when sublet to Mrs. Grace Anderson whose income failed to meet expenses.

In 1925 Ira Lute convinced the Board to allow him to rent the faltering Heights to the Rocky Mountain Artist Colony for their summer school. His request was turned down the previous year since their objectives were "not in accord with (the) aims and purposes of the Conference" according to the Board. However, by 1925 the Board decided that rental income in any form was more important than any possible harm the artists could inflict.

The obvious solution was to find a buyer for the properties. That was tried as early as 1924 without results. In January 1926 Dr. Stone returned from his world tour and offered to repurchase The Cliffs, thus solving half of the problem. Unfortunately, in the interim, the Association's cash flow was dealt a dual blow of meeting operating expenses and mortgage payments without adequate rental income.

The untimely land purchase was only part of the story. By 1924 the Association had $15,000 in unpaid bills. Rather than add it to the existing $55,000 mortgage, the Board attempted to raise the funds. The effort was met with indifference for unknown reasons and only $6,400 was pledged. Consequently, the balance was added to the debt load of the Conference.

Things continued to deteriorate in 1925 with a net loss of $14,000. Three years later that figure doubled. The Association was awash in a sea of red ink. William E. Sweet and A.A. Hyde stepped in to make personal loans of $10,000 each. The loans were conditional on the YMCA formulating a plan to seek permanent refinancing. In 1927 Ira Lute stepped down as Executive Secretary of the Association but remained on the Board of Directors. The next several years saw a quick succession of less capable managers when the Association needed stable leadership.

The downhill slide continued in 1930. The Association tried to open a girls' camp at The Heights in 1929 and 1930 but met with total failure. Five of the Heights cabins were loaded on skids, brought down the mountain, and relocated in a grove of pines. Rental of the "Tree Group" salvaged some income for the 1930 season.

In 1930 the Grocery Store was closed as a cost cutting measure. According to Secretary Black, people were arriving in their cars brought much of what they needed with them. Black entered into an agreement with Mr. Brainard of the Estes Park Market who had a man call on every occupied cottage each morning taking orders to be delivered that afternoon. A partition was put up between the Post Office and the empty grocery. The vacant space was turned into a library for the Summer School.

While the word "Depression" does not appear in official records until 1931, there were signs of serious financial problems when the holder of a $5,000 note refused to give an extension.

In July 1930 President Sweet pressed home the seriousness of the problem when he said:

> The situation... is so critical that we cannot continue to pay our overhead charges of maintenance, salaries, and interest on the mortgage debt unless sources of greatly increased revenue from operation can be found.... Unless the interest of new groups can be enlisted, as well as the increased attendance upon conferences already being held..., it is only a question of a short time before the Conference grounds will have to be permanently closed.

Next, Mr. Lute reported on his efforts to seek new financing for the Association as a condition of the Sweet/Hyde loan. He reported that none of the companies contacted "would even consider our proposal."

By the end of 1931 it was obvious that the Association was in deep trouble and even more belt tightening was needed for 1932. The laundry was closed, staffing was cut, only rented cabins were opened, and the grounds were closed on August 23. The Drug Store, Book Store, and Soda Fountain were concessioned. Business continued to decline with receipts falling to 50% of the previous year.

In February 1933 even deeper cuts were proposed by the Executive Committee. They included opening only needed cabins, shutting off one-half of the Administration Building, shutting down a portion of Wind River Lodge, opening the Assembly Hall only on Sunday and for large groups, concessioning out the Dining Hall, closing Kindernook, closing the Women's Building, and closing the bath house four days per week. The biggest cut came in staffing. Secretary Ebersole reported that in 1933 the grounds were operated with only 15 people on the payroll. The cuts were effective since at the end of the season there was a $3,000 cash surplus. As a result of the encouraging results, the Board passed a resolution to operate on a balanced budget while seeking a permanent solution.

The Cliffs House, an untimely purchase.
Lula W. Dorsey Museum

The Board Considers A Poison Pill

In 1930 Ira Lute brought up the subject of selling the Conference property to the National Park Service as a means of solving the financial problems. According to Lute the Park Service was moving to "acquire considerable acreage" asking Congress for $6,000,000 to initiate a buy out program. The idea was tempting since Dr. Stone pointed out there would be enough money to pay all the Association debts, future leases, upkeep, insurance, and continue the work of the Conference. A committee of Dr. Stone, W.A. Luke, Ira Lute and A.A. Ebersole was appointed to meet with the government's agent, Mr. Solinsky.

The committee quickly set about its task. From auditor's reports they determined that Conference property and improvements were valued at $396,000. So as not to appear greedy, the committee recommended a tentative sale price of $200,000.

With the Depression deepening and the government's funds committed to more pressing needs, money for such expenditures was nonexistent. However, the committee went forward in its crucial mission. When the Conference's financial situation reached the breaking point in 1932, the committee met with Mr. Horace Albright, Director of National Park Service, pressing him to close the deal by January 1933. In typical bureaucratic fashion, the sale was tied up in red tape. By July, the government which was running out of money tendered an offer of $80,000. The Board quickly accepted the offer even though that amount covered only mortgages and the 1932 operating deficit.

In August 1933 the sale of the property was described as "pending." In return for the land, the Conference would receive a twenty year lease and $80,000. Secretary Ebersole's salary was continued at $100 per month. All other salaries were suspended as of October 1. The sale was again delayed by red tape when it was revealed that the government could not acquire the property directly. The Conference first had to sell it to an individual who in turn would sell it to the government. This revelation set the committee off in search of someone with enough cash. John D. Rockefeller Jr. was approached but declined since his funds were already committed. Next the Phelps-Stokes and Carnegie Foundations were contacted but likewise turned down the committee's request.

When the sale stalled, the Association's financial situation reached the point of no return. There were $7,800 in unpaid bills in addition to delinquent mortgages. The official records contain dire warnings that the grounds "could be taken over at any minute" by the holder of the first mortgage, and outstanding bills "may throw the entire Conference into bankruptcy." In December 1934, A.A. Hyde once again helped by purchasing the first mortgage until the sale was closed. The mortgage holder, American Agency and Investment Company, eager to recover something, discounted the loan $13,900. The discounted amount was taken as a third mortgage to be paid when the sale closed.

A Few Shining Stars

To characterize this period of the Association's history as one disaster after another would be unfair. There were bright spots although few in number. The success of Fellowship prompted Hyde to build a companion unit. Dedicated on July 5, 1926 the House of Friendship, built from trees felled on the property, operated under the same philosophy and rules as Fellowship. Like its predecessor, Friendship was well received and filled to capacity the first season.

Camping was becoming increasingly popular and Friendship's facilities reflected that trend as a period newspaper account indicates:

> Friendship Park represents the last word in its provision for the comfort and pleasure of the visitors of the Conference Grounds who prefer camping out during their stay.

For those preferring small sleeping cabins, Hyde built two duplexes consisting of two one room cottages joined with a continuous roof with parking for two cars in between. Each cabin was equipped with a stove, table, two chairs, and folding bed. Renters were required to provide their own bedding, towels, and cooking utensils.

The Administration Building received a facelift in 1927 at the urgings of William E. Sweet and A.A. Hyde. Both were familiar with Yellowstone Lodge and its distinctive western flavor. To emulate that style, the present light fixtures, natural log supports, and animals were added to the interior.

As the Summer School faded away so did its recreational programming. In 1926 Nelson W. Benning, took a three month leave of absence from the Phoenix YMCA to fill the gap serving as program leader for the Conference. He entertained guests by "planning and leading hikes, scenic trips, and interpreting flowers and trees, ..."

One of the duplex units at Friendship.
Lula W. Dorsey Museum

A group of boys from Chicago prepare to set up camp at Friendship.
Lula W. Dorsey Museum

Progress in programming aimed at families and general guests gained strength when the Summer School completely collapsed. In 1932 "Program and Recreation" was first mentioned as a part of the Conference's offerings. Bernard Joy and his wife were employed to help groups plan programs and advise guests on the best use of time.. They scheduled lectures, concerts, plays, games, movies, and dramatic readings. In 1933, with sale of the Conference pending, the Joys were offered the free use of a cabin in exchange for their services. In that year the first organized hiking program sanctioned by the Conference appeared.

The 1920s saw the emergence of the Dorsey family as important patrons of the Association. Emily Dorsey "discovered" the YMCA in 1917 when she and a friend were vacationing in Boulder. They scheduled a day trip to Estes Park including a tour through Rocky Mountain National Park and lunch at the YMCA. Like so many others before them, they fell in love with Estes Park. The pair secured accommodations at the YMCA and telephoned Boulder ordering their baggage sent up.

Emily Dorsey returned to Estes Park in 1918 renting Barberry cabin. The next year she persuaded her father Henry Dorsey Sr., brother Henry Jr., and sister Lula to visit as well. Later that summer the senior Dorsey, daughter Lula, and Ira Lute were sitting on the Administration Building porch when Dorsey asked his daughter if she would like to have a cabin at the YMCA. After some thought, Lula Dorsey replied she would if it had electricity and running water. Lute indicated that her requests could be accommodated.

The Dorsey cabin "Outlook" was ready for the summer of 1921. Emily Dorsey who worked at an orphanage arranged to bring 21 children, a cook, and 2 matrons to Estes Park. She had Outlook, Barberry, a lean-to, and a tent to accommodate the group.

Henry Dorsey Sr. embraced the YMCA and what it stood for. He immediately took a liking to the seasonal employees especially the ones with the most menial jobs, because he felt they were the least noticed. He often rode the garbage wagon carrying a large sack of bananas. Handing them out to children, he became a Pied Piper.

Henry Dorsey Sr. on the garbage wagon.
Courtesy of Lulabeth Melton

Henry Dorsey Sr.'s wife, Lula, was not easily convinced to come to Estes Park since she was not one to rough it. When she did come to the YMCA in 1923, she too fell under the spell of the YMCA and Estes Park.

In 1927 the senior Dorsey learned of the Conference's need for additional meeting space. The name "Texas" was previously carried by one of the small meeting rooms behind the Administration Building. Being a true Texan he was not satisfied that such an insignificant building carry the name of his home state; therefore, he built the best classroom on the grounds, the "Texas Cottage."

Dorsey's interests were not limited to serious pursuits. He thought children should have a fishing lake so he built the first Dorsey Lake. Dorsey also built a foot bridge to connect the Second Mesa with the main grounds to shorten his walks between Outlook and the Administration Building. Unfortunately, his participation was cut short with his untimely death in 1928. His wife and children continued to enjoy the grounds taking an active role in the development of the Association.

Normalcy Amidst the Difficulty

For staff during the Depression, life went on as usual even though it did require some innovative methods to make ends meet. One such staffer was Ben Myers who was working his way through the University of Nebraska as barber and beautician . One of his customers worked at the YMCA the previous summer and told him she knew that there was an opening for someone with his skills the coming summer.

When Myers arrived, he was given the little one room cabin that was one of the Wind River Lodge's original buildings for his shop. One end was a barbershop and the other a beauty shop. With the Depression at its height, most people, especially staff, could not afford his services. Consequently, he worked out a punch card system to give discounts to staff. Nonetheless, many days his total take was only $.75 to a $1.50 barely covering expenses.

To make ends meet Ben Myers did a little moonlighting. In exchange for room and board he was put in charge of mopping and cleaning the bathhouse after ten o'clock each night. For spending money Myers led sunrise trail rides. Leaving around midnight after finishing his janitorial duties, he took groups up Twin Sisters on horseback. Arriving back on the grounds for breakfast, he caught a little sleep before opening his shop.

Ben Myers' adventures leading tourists up Twin Sisters whetted his appetite for a more challenging endeavor. Bud

Nelson who was working at the livery talked Myers into climbing Mt. Ypsilon. They made the ascent not by the traditional method of the north side but by going straight up the "Y" on the south face. Nelson, the stronger climber, took the lead tying Myers to him with a length of rope. Myers credited Nelson with saving his life at least three times when Myers fell, and Nelson hauled him up by the rope. When they got to the top, Mother Nature had a surprise waiting for them in the form of a summer thunderstorm. Trapped, they spent the night on top of Mt. Ypsilon under a rock ledge.

Ben Myers in his shop.
Lula W. Dorsey Museum

Ben Myers' roommate that summer was Charles Eagleplume. They were thrown together as most staff were by "luck of the draw." Eagleplume was there to run the Gift Shop. As a cost cutting measure, the Board had decided to concession the Shop. Finding a suitable concessionaire met with some difficulty. Finally, when a concessionaire was found it was the subject of an entry in the July 1931 Board Minutes:

> Just a little more than two weeks ago we were finally able to arrange with Mr. Perkins, the owner and operator of the Indian Curio Shop on the South St. Vrain road near Long's Peak Inn, to open up a branch shop in the corner of our lobby. He was able to secure the services of a young half-breed Indian, a junior at the University of Colorado, Mr. Charles Eagleplume, to take charge of this shop for us.

The one quarter Blackfoot Indian majoring in English gave the impression of being a rough character, but as Myers soon learned, Eagleplume had a soft heart. When Myers came down with the flu his roommate returned to the dorm every few hours to check on him and bring soup. When the flu persisted Eagleplume pulled out his medicine bag and proceeded to practice Native American healing arts on Myers. Ben Myers remembers that, "it must have worked because I got well!"

Like Myers, Charles Eagleplume soon found out that money was hard to come by during the summer of 1931. After selling only a few dollars of Indian goods in a couple of weeks, he hit upon the idea of getting dressed up in his full Indian regalia and putting on a show. According to Eagleplume after he and a friend put on a show one night, they passed the hat among the crowd. They collected a sizable amount for their efforts. Subsequently, the show became a regular part of the entertainment for the rest of the season.

Charles Eagleplume in his regalia.
Lula W. Dorsey Museum

During the Depression guests saw a reduction in services; however, their day to day enjoyment of the grounds went unabated. The Colvin family was typical of the period. Harold Colvin first visited Estes Park in 1925 while attending a YMCA Student Conference. Eventually, the family consisting of wife Reba, and twins, Elizabeth and Margaret, settled down in Fellowship at Agate cabin. The twins went to Kindernook and participated in its activities. Reba Colvin enjoyed hiking and nature study. Harold Colvin participated in the Summer School program and later served on the Board of Directors during the dark days of the 1930s. His leisure time was spent in fishing with his good friend, A.A. Hyde.

The family rented Agate cabin on a seasonal basis and looked upon it as their home, despite its primitive conditions. Water came from a faucet outside the door and baths for the active twins had to be taken at the Administration Building. Furniture and equipment were likewise spartan. The Colvins solved that problem by bringing additional furnishings from home.

Harold Colvin typified many of the YMCA Secretaries using the grounds. He brought his family with him to School and rented a cabin for the season. When School was over, he traveled back to the hot lowlands to resume his work. As the summer came to a close, Colvin again returned to Estes and spent his vacation. Later, the family packed up and left for the winter. They left their personal belongings in Agate cabin confident they were safe even though the cabin had no lock on the door.

Light at the End of the Tunnel

While contemplating its "poison pill," the Board had unknowingly found the solution to its problems in 1933. In a show of good faith to its creditors, the Board resolved to operate on a balanced budget until sale of the property was completed. By 1934, the wisdom of the Board's motion became apparent when there was enough surplus cash to pay off two-thirds of the delinquent bills from 1932.

By 1936 the Depression was waning and the sea of red ink was declining. There were several signs that things had turned around. The Board voted to pick up more of Secretary Evans' expenses. Also in 1936 there was first mention of "rehabilitation" of the grounds and possible refinancing of the $60,000 debt. Unfortunately, A.A. Hyde did not live to see the tide turn. He died on January 10, 1935.

In 1937, A.L. Mayer was appointed Executive Secretary. Even though Mayer's primary responsibility was with the West Central Area Council of the YMCA, he brought strong leadership missing since the departure of Ira Lute. Business continued to improve in 1937. The first payment was made on the Hyde/Sweet loan of 1930. That year saw 13 cabins changed from canvas shades to glass windows. New tools were purchased and repairs were made on long neglected facilities.

The last mention of selling the property occurred on August 29, 1937 when local grocer and Board member, Fay Brainard, indicated he doubted the negotiated twenty year lease back was renewable. Brainard further stated he "knew of some cases where the leases expired and the land was thrown back to its natural state." It was a psychological turning point for the Conference. The Board decided that an uncertain future was preferable to none at all.

The Board quickly focused its attention on consolidating and refinancing the Conference's $58,900 in mortgages. The Hyde estate was anxious to close out the first mortgage. The University of Wichita was equally anxious to settle its share of the Hyde/Sweet loan left to it by Hyde. Sweet remained unpaid as well. With money still in short supply, the Board turned to the federal government's Reconstruction Finance Corporation. Unfortunately, the Association's financial position was too sound to receive federal aid. Then the Board considered selling 500 shares to individuals at $100 each, but that was dropped since the Board could not find the required number of people.

More signs of an improving economy appeared in 1938. The Board approved a 10% increase in rental rates. They appropriated $1,800 for improvements meeting with disapproval by Secretary Mayer who had requested $5,500. At the August Board meeting, it was voted to bring all interest and principal payments up to date on the first and second mortgages. Any cash surpluses were applied to repairs.

The Board's perseverance during the Depression was rewarded in 1938 when it was informed that business was "getting back to normal." They received an additional pat on the back by the Employed Officers Conference which had replaced the traditional Summer School. They expressed their appreciation for the fine treatment they had received during their conference.

In 1939 J.J. McConnell, Executive of the Southwest Area temporarily took over for an ailing Mayer. This provided the Conference with continued professional leadership. It ushered in an era whereby the affairs of the Conference were looked after jointly by the West Central Area and the Southwest Area. The boards of the two areas were responsible for electing the Conference Board and providing an executive to run the Conference on a seasonal basis.

Business continued to improve in 1939 when the long ailing conference business showed signs of improvement. The usual conferences were increasing in numbers of delegates. There were new conferences including the United Presbyterian National Convention attended by 800 persons and the International Council of Religious Education bringing 600 people to the grounds.

As the 1930s came to a close prospects for the future seemed bright. For the first time in many years capital expenditures were discussed to improve accommodations and guests' services. The first mortgage owed to Hyde's heirs and the second owed to the University of Wichita were refinanced through the United States National Bank of Denver. Improvements to the grounds included new sidewalks, oiling of roads, purchasing new beds and mattresses, remodeling of cabins, and long needed painting.

In 1940 A.L. Mayer returned to his position as Executive Secretary. The annual audit showed a net excess revenue of $5,158. He stated that for the first time since before the Depression the Conference was current on all bills. In 1941 the conference business was down slightly, but for the first time in many years, cabins were full to capacity for the entire season. After years of struggle, the Board seemed to have acquired a fanatical aversion to debt; so most of the cash surplus was applied to paying off the Conference debt.

Casualties of the Depression

The Conference had survived the Depression, but there were casualties. For many, the saddest loss was the closing of Fellowship and Friendship. The Depression aside, the demise of Friendship and Fellowship was due in part to the departure of Ira Lute as Executive Secretary. With his leaving, the communities lost one of their staunchest supporters. The succeeding Secretaries were ambivalent at best to Friendship and Fellowship. One particular administrator viewed the primitive handmade furniture and equipment as a liability rather than an asset. In 1934 Friendship and Fellowship fell victim to a series of belt tightening proposals when the matron in charge of both was dismissed. Both properties were then made available to conference groups on a short term rental basis. Consequently, all traces of the community disappeared except for the buildings and the memories.

In August 1937 the Women's Auxiliary ceased to exist when a formal motion to disband was made. The Women's Building, Kindernook and the treasury containing $23.38 were turned over to the Association. The Women's Auxiliary had made a valiant struggle for survival. Dues were collected, dishes purchased, and improvements were made to the building through the 1932 season.

The failure of the Auxiliary was as much a result of a change in attitudes as was the Depression. The group and its facilities had served three primary functions: child care, women's programming, and social center for the Conference. With child care and social functions taken over by the Association and women welcome at the new Employed Officers Conference, the reasons for the Women's Auxiliary were gone.

The Estes Park Conference had survived failure of the Summer School, untimely and unwise expenditures, and the Depression. The Association's finances were in a shambles with an enormous debt load. Without the School's resource pool, guest programming was on a catch as catch can basis. Facilities were in a total state of disrepair from self imposed neglect. However, the Association had survived its greatest crisis.

The 1940s: Decade of Change

Failure of the Summer School had left a large void in the spirit of the Estes Park Conference not to mention an equally large number of empty beds, but the prevailing attitude was a positive one. While the Estes Park Conference was coming into the light, the clouds of war had already darkened the skies of Europe and Asia. Soon, the United States and the Association were dragged into the conflagration. At the end of World War II the Association entered a period of change as the post-war bookings filled beds and strained facilities.

The Conference Goes on a Wartime Footing

With the United States fighting for its survival, the Conference did its part in the war effort by keeping the grounds "open as a center for rest and relaxation in getting away from the worry of war stress." Advertising took on a patriotic appeal stating that:

> When every day away from the job means a loss in manpower; when transportation is at a premium; when many former vacation routines are out; when everything, even vacation, must contribute to winning of the war, thousands of Americans will seek a vacation opportunity in 1944 which will offer both recreation and inspiration to the entire family.

Although many difficulties were encountered, the Conference managed to hold its own during the conflict due in part to capable leadership. Going into the conflict, leadership was provided by A.L. Mayer. In 1942 the West Central Area and Southwest Area Councils began sharing responsibility for the Conference with each electing one-third of the Estes Park Board and providing one professional staff member to manage the Conference.

By the summer of 1942 it became readily apparent that the war would have a major impact on the Conference. Cancellations turned a $10,000 surplus in 1941 into a $5,000 deficit in 1942. The drastic drop in rental income was blamed on gas rationing and inability to secure space on trains whose first priority was transporting troops and supplies. Lack of adequate transportation was dismissed in wartime advertising stating:

> You don't need a car. Most people will be coming by train and bus. That's the way it always used to be. Many of the finest hikes can be taken directly from camp, and the longer ones on horseback. Our extensive equipment and facilities make it unnecessary to leave camp.

Coping with the obstacles of war fell primarily on the shoulders of Harper Glezen and Sam Schreiner, who as Area Executives, were given the responsibility of running the Association.

Despite the difficulties the Board of Directors "felt that an optimistic view should be taken of the future and plans made for operating in 1943 on the same terms as the past." That was easier said than done. With several hundred mouths to feed, food rationing presented a major hurdle. Meat and sugar were impossible to get; chickens, however, were not rationed. But due to favoritism showed by wholesalers to their year 'round customers, chickens were impossible to obtain in quantity.

Glezen noticed that farmers near Loveland had lots of chickens. He had a cage built on the back of a truck which was driven from farm to farm buying chickens for a dollar each. The chickens were placed in a pen behind the kitchen until needed. Obtaining the chickens solved only part of the problem. The staff was canvassed for someone with experience in cleaning chickens. No one seemed to know how or wanted to learn. Finally, a farm girl from Kansas was found who had watched her father dress chickens.

Food rationing necessitated other creative measures on the part of management. Ration points were allocated on the basis of the number of meals served the previous month. Margaret Landon, who was in charge of kitchen, came up with a novel way to add to the Conference's points. Every evening she fried fresh donuts which could be smelled all over the grounds. Since a bona fide meal consisted of two food items and beverage, she served a scoop of ice cream, a donut and a cup of coffee.

The unavailability of meat precipitated one of Harper Glezen's most vivid memories of the war years. One September, after the grounds had closed, local grocer Ron Brodie called and during the course of the conversation asked how many employees were still there. Glezen responded that there were eight including himself closing the grounds before winter. A little later Brodie showed up with eight large t-bone steaks. Glezen remembered that those were the first steaks he had seen in two years and the best he ever ate!

Regardless of the financial reversals resulting from the War, the Board continued its efforts to reduce the Conference indebtedness. The $13,900 lien against the property by the American Agency and Investment Company arising out of the defaulted mortgage during the Depression was finally settled for $750. By the beginning of 1943 the Conference's total obligations were cut to $20,000.

As the clouds of war continued to darken, problems associated with the conflict mounted. With most men in uniform, there were problems filling positions traditionally assigned to men. High school boys were used in capacities where women were deemed physically unable to do the job. Reminiscent of the Depression, positions were consolidated and the grounds operated "short staffed." Sam Schreiner and Harper Glezen took turns working as night watchmen, mopping the bathrooms, and sweeping the Administration Building. The watchman's last assignment was to go to the kitchen at 5 a.m. where the old Army coal stove required stoking before the cook arrived.

When the livery concessionaire fell ill and his sons volunteered for the armed service, the responsibility for opening the livery fell upon Glezen. He scoured the Valley for surplus horses but met with only minimal success. With the help of a local horseman, Glezen went to a horse auction in Denver where a suitable number were purchased; however, there still was not anyone to run the stable. Glezen added that to his list of duties. His secretary, Ellen Stoddard, often had to take dictation as Glezen saddled horses and cleaned the stable.

In 1943 with the tide of war just turning in favor of the Allies, some forward looking people were already anticipating peace. The Superintendent of Rocky Mountain National Park predicted "that there would be a tremendous increase in tourist and vacation business after the war." The Board agreed stating "that we must be prepared..." for peace and resolved:

> It is the conviction of all those present that the religious, educational and recreational purposes for which the Camp was founded are as pertinent and essential today as they ever were and that the Camp should play an important part in the reconstruction and the building of world peace.

In 1944, with victory in sight, usage of the grounds increased over the previous year in spite of continuing travel difficulties, rationing, and personnel problems.

By the time the grounds opened for business in 1945, the war in Europe had ended. As the season waned, victory over Japan loomed on the horizon, but still it came unexpectedly. August 14 was like most other summer days for Elizabeth Dorsey. Her family had gone up Trail Ridge Road but in characteristic teenage fashion, she decided to stay back at camp to "hang out" with her friends, Katie Bell, Joe Bell, Bill Hawes,

Lynn Helm, Jane Helm, John McDowell, Max Schreiner, and Stan Schreiner.

The teenagers staked out a spot on the Post Office porch where the half log railings made a perfect perch. Stan Schreiner was strumming his ukulele when one of their friends came running over from the Administration Building yelling that the war was over. Euphoric, the kids started honking horns of cars parked in front of the Administration Building. Liz Dorsey made a beeline for the rope attached to the bell atop the Administration Building and rang it deliriously.

Her brother-in-law Troy Acord and his family were in the National Park when they learned the news. Lieutenant Acord, in uniform, was on leave from 2nd Air Force Headquarters in Colorado Springs. Having taken his family on their favorite drive up Trail Ridge, they were coming down and had just passed Rainbow Curve, when a man coming from the opposite direction flagged them down. The man leaned out his window and hollered, "Hey soldier, did you know the war was over? Turn on your radio. It's on all the stations." That night the Acords joined everyone in the Valley dancing the night away in downtown Estes Park. Thus, the 1945 season ended with a well deserved upswing of spirit.

The Post War Boom

At the onset of World War II, the Conference facilities were in desperate condition from years of neglect. With prospects for increased business at the conclusion of the conflict, the Conference was faced with the dual problem of upgrading existing facilities and providing new ones. To accomplish this, the Board resolved to raise $100,000 to coincide with the centennial of the YMCA in North America in 1954. The Southwest Area, West Central Area, and Estes Park Conference would share equally in raising the funds. Even with help of the Areas, the campaign never reached a successful conclusion and was eventually discontinued.

War weary Americans returned en masse to the YMCA of the Rockies.
Lula W. Dorsey Museum   F.P. Clatworthy Jr.

One can imagine the delight of Board and management in assembling the first "wish list" in years. With dining facilities limited to 100 while there were sleeping accommodations for several hundred, an expanded Dining Hall topped the list. A new lodge also appeared on the list since management indicated they could easily rent twice the number of lodge rooms available in Wind River Lodge.

Third on the list was a house of worship. Construction of a church in memory of A.A. Hyde was proposed shortly after his death in 1935, but was delayed while the Conference sorted out its problems. His family and friends again suggested building a church in Hyde's memory as a part of the Centennial Fund.

Last on the list was additional staff housing. Seasonal employee housing was already occupying space that could be rented to guests. Any expansion in guest facilities would require additional staff, compounding the problem.

With post war prosperity at hand, the Board, in characteristic fashion, authorized the borrowing of $60,000 to begin work even before any money was raised. Some funds were quickly diverted to purchasing property considered vital to the interest of the Conference. In late 1945, Lower Hyde and companion cabins were purchased for $5,000 from Friends University of Wichita which had received them from George Hyde.

Spring 1946 saw the Conference grounds a beehive of activity with a variety of projects underway. Not all the projects were completed as planned. The Hyde Memorial Church was put on hold until funds were available. Instead of a new lodge, additional cabins and a new shower house were built at Friendship. Food for small conferences was transported from the Kitchen and served in the Friendship Community House.

To solve food service problems an annex to the Dining Room was built. The Pine Room increased seating capacity to 300. The kitchen was unable to handle the increased capacity so it was remodeled. Part of the updating included an automatic, oil fired boiler installed across the street in the maintenance building. Unfortunately, a pipe fitter had not properly installed an expansion joint which converted the basement storage area into a sauna steaming the labels off all the cans! Fortunately, the chef remembered what was stored where so there were only a few surprises.

Employees benefitted from construction of the Mummy Quadrangle including three dormitories and an employee recreation hall. Harper Glezen contacted the man who had the contract for cutting on Colorado State Forest lands and purchased several large truck loads of lumber. With construction materials in short supply, the trucks caused quite a commotion as they made their way through town.

The three dormitories and the recreation hall were arranged in a square facing a central courtyard and joined by a fence. Management felt it important that they could report to parents their children were under close supervision. Thus, the staff counselors whose apartment was in the Recreation Hall closely monitored the comings and goings of the staff.

The new Pine Room.
Lula W. Dorsey Museum

Bertha and Jim DeLuna (left) prepare to serve a smorgasbord.
Lula W. Dorsey Museum   P.D. Houston

The improvements came none too soon as the YMCA experienced one of its busiest seasons in 1946. Conference groups increased from eight in 1945 to 37. Family cabins were filled before the season opened except for the first two weeks in June. All facilities were taxed to the limit with an average of 600 persons using the grounds daily.

The crush of vacation hungry Americans exposed a major weakness in shared management of the Association by the Southwest and West Central Areas. The affairs of the Conference required a full time manager. Consequently, in 1946 Lisle T. Ware became the first full time Resident Director of the Association working under the direction of the Areas.

Another weakness exposed by the flood of tourists was the lack of a cabin reservation policy. By the 1947 season the Conference had developed a membership program that was tied to a new reservation policy. Members were given first priority in renting accommodations, followed by members of other local Associations, then ministers and church officials, and lastly former guests. Preference was given to families over individuals and to full season rentals over shorter stays.

In 1947 the Conference continued to purchase additional property. Three rental cabins, Dream, Nymph and Hiyaha sitting on three acres, were purchased from Jack Woods. Nymph Cabin, as its name implies, was very small. Conference Registrar George Gay had received numerous requests for a honeymoon cabin and Nymph seemed to fit the bill. When the first two honeymooning couples both checked out after staying only one night, Gay went to investigate. Opening the door he found that Housekeeping had made up the cabin with a bunk bed thinking it too small for a double bed!

In 1949 the Association purchased Rainbow Ranch, consisting of the Ranch House and Dude Rooms, for $24,000. Although relations with its present owner were cordial, a previous owner was a continual source of irritation with numerous late night disturbances. When the Ranch came up for sale the Conference moved quickly. The loan balance was paid off in five years with rental income from conference groups.

Demands on the Conference made by private cabin owners had long been a point of concern. In an extension of its policy of purchasing property to protect the interest of the Conference, the Board moved to abolish the sale of property to individuals. Additionally it adopted a policy of exercising its first right of refusal when private property became available. In 1949 Trail's End Cabin was the first one repurchased under the new policy.

In July 1948 architect Gordon Sweet presented plans for an addition to the Administration Building housing a new soda fountain. The Rustic Room was open for business in 1949 despite being built under extreme weather conditions. Snowdrifts four to ten feet deep and winds so intense that several cabins were blown off their foundations prompted the Maintenance Superintendent to describe the winter as "being the most severe in Estcs Park history." Finished in knotty pine paneling the new soda fountain was an instant success. Included in the project was a remodeled gift shop and office space. Knotty pine paneling matching the Rustic Room was added to the Administration Building lobby.

Guests enjoy the newly acquired Thompson Ranch (Ranch House).
Lula W. Dorsey Museum

The new Mummy Quadrangle.
Lula W. Dorsey Museum

Serving up sodas to thirsty guests in the new Rustic Room.
Lula W. Dorsey Museum

Cabins Receive Needed Attention

While the Conference had made progress in many areas, its cabins described as "rustic" in advertising were viewed as run down and primitive by many guests. Most cabins still had wood burning stoves necessitating lessons for new guests lest they burn down the cabin. Iceboxes were seen as just plain backward. Tar paper did little to keep out cold, wind, and dirt. Celotex partitions were stained and full of holes. Decades old wood floors were so rough they had to be hosed down and swept rather than mopped. Worst of all some cabins still lacked indoor bathrooms. Some guests renting the same cabin for the entire season every year began their own program of modernization by bringing old refrigerators and furniture from home.

Updating existing cabins went a long way toward adding to the comfort of guests, but the ultimate solution was to build new cabins with modern conveniences. In 1941 Harold Colvin offered to build a new cabin in Fellowship. In return, he would lease the cabin for one dollar per year for twenty years after which it reverted to the Conference. The Board was caught without a policy to cover the contingency. Referred to the Executive Committee, the proposal was tabled. After the war, with demand for cabins increasing, a Conference patron was approached to build a new cabin as an example for others. When the patron declined, the idea went into limbo.

With the decade coming to a close, the Elmer Magee family took the lead in building new cabins for the Conference. In the spring of 1949 ground was broken for Twin Pines providing the first new cabin for the Association since construction of the "Japanese Indian" cabins in 1923. Lula W. Dorsey followed closely with LuHenDor cabin dedicated the next summer. With both families receiving priority in renting "their" cabins for a specific period of time, Twin Pines and LuHenDor were the beginning of the Cabin Donor Program that blossomed during the coming decades.

Wrens Nest cabin in the 1940s.
Lula W. Dorsey Museum

Evolution in Programming

During the 1940s programming took on a new direction. With the Summer School gone, the first attempts at programming directed toward the general guest population occurred during the Depression. During World War II guest programming received an enormous boost when Otto Dillner was hired as the first Program Director of the Conference.

One of Dillner's first moves was to hire Alfred Wands to give art lessons in exchange for use of a cabin. Wands was paid for adult lessons while children's classes were free. Since Wands was an avid fly fisherman, Program received the added bonus of having someone to teach fly casting. Dillner expanded other areas including hiking. To keep guests informed of the Conference offerings, the first Program Bulletin was published on a weekly basis in 1945.

Knowing that the post-war years would see a huge increase in demand for Program services, Dillner presented the Board with the first Program Department "wish list." He cited the need for program activities for children ages 7 to 15 as well as additional personnel and equipment for older teens. He also requested adequate means for transportation to trailheads for the hiking program. Dillner's request for an expanded children's program evidently went against the grain of some Board members since the 1945 minutes recorded the following:

> The policy in the past, with exception of kindergarten, has been to provide program on a family level, expecting children to be under the supervision of their parents and to participate in program with them. If specialized program for children's groups of various ages is developed further, this family policy begins to break down and the camp assumes more and more responsibility for children which has been kept with parents in the past.

In spite of initial objections, the Conference found itself taking on additional responsibility for guests' children as the years passed.

Dillner made quick progress in developing the Program Department. In 1946, he reported that expanded crafts, hiking, and children's programs were highly successful. The next year Dillner reported favorably on increased attendance at cookouts, steak fries, and overnight camping. Despite the Board's reluctance, a storage area underneath the Administration Building was turned into a teenage program area including a ping-pong table. Dillner's efforts met with success since he reported that, "again and again guests have commented on the program as the factor which has made Estes different from the average summer resort."

With the Conference quickly evolving into a family vacation camp, it needed a YMCA person experienced in camping and family programming. In 1947 Bernard Timmerman was hired as Managing Director. He quickly accelerated Program development by hiring Ned Linegar as Program Director. With 14 years experience at George Williams College Camp, Timmerman said Linegar was "the best program person in the whole YMCA movement."

During the next three years changes in programming quickened. The hangout underneath the Administration Building which was primarily used by roughhousing teenagers was remodeled in 1948. The facelift included a jukebox and knotty pine paneling with western cattle brands burned into the walls. The kids named it the "Gopher Hole." Dick Drabble was hired as livery master to expand offerings past the mere renting of horses. Drabble began giving riding lessons to children to promote the western aura of the Conference and introduced steak fry rides.

Timmerman's last year, 1950, saw a veritable explosion in Programming. The Estes Park Folk Festival was held with children, teenagers, and adults given the opportunity to learn all types of ethnic, classical, and folk dances. A new Day Camp for 7 to 14 year olds was highly successful serving 35 to 40 children per day. Kindernook was expanded to provide both morning and afternoon child care. Dick Drabble sponsored a 4th of July Indian ceremony and riding show as well as Indian Campfire ceremonies each Saturday night. Music Directors Betty Hutton and Barbara Parks brought in the Rocky Ridge Music Center for concerts. The first Arts and Crafts Festival was held in the Administration Building.

Success was, as always, a two edged sword. The quality of programs prompted townspeople, private cabin owners, and other non-guests to attend programs. Existing facilities were strained beyond the breaking point. Linegar and Timmerman pointed out that if Program was to continue to be successful, buildings specifically dedicated for that purpose were a necessity.

Shuffleboard on the Administration Building porch.
Lula W. Dorsey Museum

Miniature golf in the 1940s.
Lula W. Dorsey Museum

The Gopher Hole under the Administration Building.
Lula W. Dorsey Museum

Conferences Rebound

The fortunes of the Association became more closely linked
to that of conference groups during the 1940s. When the Estes
Park Conference was hard hit with cancellations in 1942, it was
due in large part to lessened group business. Even though
conference business was down, the Board stuck to its policy of
limiting groups to "YMCAs, churches, schools, conference
groups, and individuals related to such groups...." Later the
Board realized that restricting conference business to such
groups was self limiting so discussed seeking conferences in the
areas of art, music, and literature. During the war, the Board
heard reports of tremendous pent up demand on the part of
conferences, but as with cabin guests, the limiting factor was the
availability of transportation.

As the tide of war turned, conference groups kept pace with
the upturn in family cabin business. In 1945, twenty-one

conferences were served, up thirteen from the previous year, with ten being turned away because of lack of space. At the conclusion of the war, group business began to boom in earnest. New groups such as The Estes Park Conference on Human Relations in Industry sponsored by the West Central Area Council of the YMCA started in 1946. Its theme was "Christian Principles Working in Employer-Employee Relations." As might be expected, family reunions became a significant growth area as families renewed ties interrupted by war.

Conference groups such as the Consumers Cooperative Association or COOP endured the same primitive living conditions as did cabin guests. Twenty years later those conditions were recalled:

> Tho accommodations at this camp at that time were far from deluxe. They had one-story... barracks, built-in partitions. Army cots and pads - no mattresses. Some... recall that the first order of the day, after (receiving)... assignment to the barracks, was collecting batches of newspapers to stop up the knotholes. ...The only toilet facilities were at the back of the Administration Building.

For a few, the conditions were too rustic. Some "would-be campers would take one look at the facilities and were gone...." However, those who stayed began "to get into the pioneer spirit and proceeded to enjoy themselves." Pioneering spirit was not limited to living conditions. During the war, with the Association running short staffed, the COOPs "were split into three groups and each group took one day to be responsible for peeling potatoes, getting the food ready for the cooks, and being waiters and waitresses...."

The old Summer School spirit endured in the Association of Secretaries conference for employed officers of the YMCA. The AOS provided a variety of courses including seminars, short courses, and clinic sessions. Twelve day courses offering college credit through George Williams University were directed at YMCA Junior Secretaries needing courses for certification. In the spirit of the old School, platform speakers of note challenged conferees to strive for excellence, and a special program was developed for wives of employed officers.

As the 1940s came to a close, the Estes Park Conference found itself relying more and more on groups as a source of revenue. Unpredictable fluctuations in conference attendance sometimes left the Association with empty beds. As a result, the Board moved to establish standard policies pertaining to group reservations with guaranteed numbers and deposits.

At the Brink of a Renaissance

By the time the 1940s drew to a close, the Association had shed the last vestiges of the Summer School. Soon the old YMCA "camp" image disappeared to be replaced with that of a modern family resort and conference center. The Association truly was poised at the brink of a Renaissance.

The Ruesch Years

The hiring of Walter G. Ruesch as Managing Director in 1950 ushered in a new era for the Estes Park Conference. He began his YMCA career in Wisconsin and later joined the West Central Area YMCA staff managing four separate camps. Ruesch intended to stay in Estes Park for only three years lest he gain the reputation as a "camp man." He faced a multitude of problems. However, the Conference possessed a solid YMCA tradition of serving families, conferences, and staff. Ruesch spent the next three decades accentuating those strengths by building new accommodations and program facilities for conferences and families.

Ruesch Makes a Bold Proposal

Walter Ruesch arrived on the grounds during mid summer of 1950. He quickly began assessing the Conference operations before officially assuming his job in October. Ruesch found facilities in "deplorable" condition. To bring facilities up to acceptable standards required an infusion of capital not available from a three month "camp" operation; therefore, he proposed to begin year around operations. Ruesch projected that after winterizing the Mummy Quadrangle, off season use would net $500 per weekend for 10 weekends the first year. When Maintenance Superintendent Ken Miller heard the proposal he said, "It can't be done." Some Board members were just as skeptical; however, they approved the proposition if it could be accomplished at an expenditure of $2,500 or less.

By April 1952 everything was "ready" when the Westminster College Fellowship arrived for the first off season conference. It was a jerry-rigged affair at best. The employee Recreation Hall served as the dining room and meeting facility. The staff counselor's office was converted into a kitchen. Mr. Ruesch drove up from Denver and worked as cook, dishwasher, and housekeeper while living in unheated Bide-A-Wee cabin.

Winterization meant more than just insulating and heating buildings. With pipes on top of the ground or scarcely below, an adequate winter water supply was the biggest obstacle to overcome. Board member Herb Willborn helped by donating a 3000 gallon redwood water tank.

The next year, Ruesch reported that "winter camp" was a rousing success with 18 groups accommodated. There were some hitches, however. Hauling water from town to fill the water tank was laborious. The makeshift kitchen arrangement kept Ruesch working from 5 a.m. till past midnight. Consequently, in 1953 two wells were drilled and a portion of the kitchen was partitioned off to make a winter kitchen. The staff dining room (Pine Room Annex) was remodeled and winterized for conference use. At the August 1953 Board meeting, Ruesch announced, "the operation of the Camp is a little different now from what it has been in the past. ...We are operating almost the year round now."

The winter camp experiment received a big boost in 1954 when Hidden Valley was designated as a Winter Sports Area. Ruesch stated that the Association "should be making plans so we can meet the needs of the various groups that may want to use our facilities." The ski area gave the Conference a new marketing tool for the off season thus expanding the number and types of groups served.

Upgrading Rustic Cabins

One of the many hurdles Ruesch faced was the condition of the Conference cabins. Years later he remembered that "those old cabins were fine for people who had been coming for years, but there just weren't enough old timers." Some new guests cut their visits short after seeing their rustic accommodations and paying Ruesch a visit to complain. Ruesch reasoned, "something had to be done in a hurry or we would lose out."

In July 1951 the Solzman family provided funds to remodel cabin #7 (Robins Nest) as an example of what could be done with the old housekeeping cabins. Remodeling included new linoleum, knotty pine paneling, shower, lavatory, hot water, and a used refrigerator. For their contribution, the Solzmans received first priority in making reservations. Anekus and Hyde-Away cabins were remodeled in similar fashion using operating surpluses.

The refurbished cabins were well received. Board members asked the West Central and Southwest Areas to assist in the program. The Lincoln YMCA immediately committed to remodeling one cabin. Other Conference supporters followed suit. Miss Lula Dorsey, Henry Dorsey Jr., Mr. and Mrs. H.L. Dannen, and Mrs. Charles Mannschreck contributed $1,000 each to remodel cabins, but with over 100 cabins on the rental charts there was a long way to go.

Remodeling the rest of the Association's cabins was going to be costly with the price of building materials riding the crest of a post war inflationary wave. To remodel the authorized number of cabins and stay within the budget was impossible. Ruesch employed a forester to survey the Conference property and harvest selected trees which were sent to Griffith Lumber. However, that yielded only a small amount of lumber. To obtain lumber in quantity at an affordable price, Ruesch dealt directly with mills on the west coast.

Other supplies presented a more formidable obstacle. As luck would have it, Ruesch made the acquaintance of Chick Dibrell who started vacationing at the YMCA in 1951. In conversation Ruesch expounded on the enormity of the task and the amount of materials required. Dibrell remembered that "in those days Walt only knew two prices - free or wholesale." Dibrell just happened to know someone who owned a hardware supply business in Galveston, Texas. Arrangements were made to ship carload lots to Lyons.

One of the "Japanese Indian" cabins, circa 1951.
Lula W. Dorsey Museum

With a guaranteed supply of materials, an enthusiastic constituency, and support of the Board, the cabin remodeling program blossomed. To handle the work, a full time carpenter was hired; however, Ruesch lent a hand by hanging towel bars and toilet paper holders. By the end of 1956 almost 60 cabins were remodeled including six for winter use. The Conference's efforts were rewarded with a higher demand for its refurbished accommodations. The Board moved quickly to finish the remaining one-third before 1960.

Refurbishing cabins was not the total answer to modernizing cabin accommodations. Ruesch realized that new cabins were the missing link. He developed a floor plan for a two bedroom cabin but lacked the funds for even one. In 1953 Lula Dorsey and her brother Henry Dorsey Jr. ushered in the modern era of cabin construction by donating funds for Tejas and Valley View cabins based on Ruesch's floor plan.

Improving Conference Accommodations

The condition of group housing was as bad or worse than that of family accommodations. In a statement to the Executive Committee, Ruesch summed up the state of group housing when he reported, "our conference facilities are in disgraceful condition and inasmuch as our main sources of revenue come from conferences, it is necessary that we do some work on these units." The units he referred to were Halletts and Ypsilon, now known as Pioneer and Fern-Odessa. When built in 1921, they were the Conference's deluxe accommodations. Years of use and neglect had left the buildings with rotted floors and pockmarked celotex partitions.

In July 1951 Ruesch asked the Board to remodel the lodges but was turned down. One year later funds were appropriated to remodel Ypsilon as an experiment. Improvements included knotty pine paneling, linoleum, baths, and general repairs. The improvements were well received, and the Board authorized improving Halletts in a similar fashion. In November 1951 Ruesch reported to the Board that work was progressing well on the lodge renamed Fern-Odessa Lodge. The 1953 conference load was heavy with 70 groups using the grounds. Many positive comments were received by returning groups on the improved accommodations. With groups already booking for the 1955 season, the Board approved remodeling Halletts and renaming it Pioneer Lodge.

With winter business booming, it became apparent that a winter lodge was needed. In July 1957 Halletts Lodge was completed at a cost of $57,000. It was none too soon as the Managing Director's report of 1958 indicated that 100 groups were served between Labor Day and Memorial Day. There were only three open weekends during the winter and there were even some mid-week bookings. To accommodate the increasing number of groups both on and off season Alpen Inn was constructed at a cost of $250,000. Dedicated on July 31, 1961, it was considered the Conference's deluxe lodge. Group accommodations were further enhanced in 1964 with the completion of Howard Hall and Hague House.

Ranch House and Four Winds were remodeled into housekeeping cabins for family reunions. They became an instant hit. Family reunions amounting to only three or four groups in 1964 jumped to 23 the next year.

The YMCA Acquires a Landmark

In 1955 the Association learned that Mountainside Lodge was for sale. Relations with the current owners were amicable, but previous proprietors had offended the sensibilities of the YMCA with racing horses, speeding cars, and rowdy parties. The Lodge along with 53 acres and accompanying cabins: Beacon Hill, Bambi, Bison, and Bighorn Annex was purchased and added greatly to the Conference's holdings.

Along with the real property the Association fell heir to the rich heritage of the Lodge built by Dr. John Timothy Stone. He had picked Estes Park as his summer home where he could reach out to young men through the YMCA and find solitude to write monographs on educational and religious themes.

Born in Boston in 1868 he graduated from Auburn Theological Seminary becoming an ordained Presbyterian Minister in 1894. Preaching from the pulpit of the Fourth Presbyterian Church in Chicago he was in great demand as a speaker, especially at universities. His enthusiasm for evangelism and his contagious zeal were probably his greatest gifts leading to his involvement in the YMCA. Stone was a tireless speaker. Once, while serving as Chaplain at Camp Grant in Rockford, Illinois during World War I, he spoke to 2,500 men giving nine different addresses at nine places in one night.

Dr. Stone was always well prepared for his sermons; however, he was not above preaching about simple things. One day he was to preach in the Assembly Hall at Estes Park when he saw a Mariposa Lily. Stone stopped and picked it deciding the simple beauty of the Lily and of God's creation would be the subject of his sermon.

The exact timetable for construction of the Mountainside Lodge is lost, but some fragmentary information has survived. The land was part of the original LaCoste homestead purchased by the YMCA. Because of its isola-

Dr. John Timothy Stone.
Lula W. Dorsey Museum

tion on the side of Emerald Mountain, it was not considered valuable to the Conference and was sold to Dr. Stone in 1917. Construction Foreman George Wiard recalled that Dr. Stone's study was built first and housed the four or five workers. Wiard's family lived in the barn (Recreation Hall). All of the logs were cut on site taking two years to finish. Stone took a cue from Enos Mills using naturally gnarled and fire killed trees. The hand of an unknown master stone mason is evident throughout the Lodge.

After using the Lodge for only three years, Stone sold it in 1924 in preparation for a world tour. The Lodge passed through numerous owners during the next 32 years. One of the most enduring stories concerning the property occurred in 1935 while it was owned by John J. Bittel and leased to Bertha Allsebrook for a girls' camp. Allsebrook and her daughter Elaine lived in Dr. Stone's old study west of the Lodge. One day Elaine and her mother went riding. When they returned the cabin was in ruins. Presumably, a spark from the fireplace had ignited a polar bear rug. Mrs. Allsebrook's wedding ring was lost in the fire and remained so despite a diligent search. As the years passed the diamond grew in size and importance until it reached gargantuan proportions in the minds of those telling the story, but as Elaine later recalled "the diamond was really quite small."

After the YMCA purchased the Lodge it was designated as group housing for conferences. Later, the Lodge and its outbuildings became a popular facility for family reunions. Situated at 8,700 feet, Mountainside offers a commanding view of the surrounding peaks.

The newly completed Mountainside Lodge.
Lula W. Dorsey Museum   F.P. Clatworthy

Mrs. Stone enjoys the living room at Mountainside.
Lula W. Dorsey Museum   F.P. Clatworthy

Ruins of Kybo, Dr. Stone's study, which conceal a diamond ring.
Colorado State Historical Society #1046

Hyde Memorial Becomes a Reality

Shortly after A.A. Hyde's death in 1935, his daughter, Pattie Hyde Barclay, proposed building a house of worship memorializing her father. The Depression put a damper on any such plans. She again broached the subject in 1943. In July 1948, architect Gordon Sweet presented elevation sketches for the proposed Hyde Memorial Church. The plans depicted a beautiful native stone and log church. When the Board learned that construction costs were in the neighborhood of $250,000 and with only $10,000 raised, construction was delayed yet again.

Renovation of the existing Assembly Hall presented a cheaper alternative. During a two year remodeling, a drop ceiling, venetian blinds, new floor, and lights were installed. The front of the building was altered by addition of a chancel and bell tower. On July 21, 1957, the Dannen Chapel located underneath the chancel was dedicated in memory of H.L. Dannen by his family Mrs. H. L. Dannen, Mr. and Mrs. Dwight Dannen, and Mr. and Mrs. Charles Mannschreck.

Henry Dorsey Jr. provided the finishing touch by donating a bell purchased from an antique shop in Texas. Hoisting "Duke" into the belfry proved a arduous task. After several hours of work, "Duke" was in place. When the bell pealed out its clear note reverberating from the mountains, adults, children, and dogs came running to find out what the commotion was about.

With dedication of Hyde Memorial, the Association not only memorialized a man who was so dedicated to the purposes of the YMCA, it finally had a house of worship. Its use, like the old Assembly Hall, was not limited to religious functions; it provided additional meeting space for conference groups and program activities as well.

Making Hyde Memorial a reality.
Lula W. Dorsey Museum

Celebrating A Golden Anniversary

In 1957 the Estes Park Conference celebrated its 50th Anniversary. It was a time to reflect on the past, rejoice in the progress of the present, and prepare for the future. In 1955 a special committee began planning activities. Sam J. Schreiner wrote <u>The Story of the Estes Park Conference</u>. All the Conference's printed material was coordinated to reflect the celebration.

The week of July 14 through 21 was set aside for the celebration. A hike commemorating the founders' trek from Grand Lake to Bear Lake was led by Garland Matthews. A program of historical sketches written by Louis Moore with accompanying music by Dan Brickley was presented. There was an old timer's coffee, chuckwagon supper, and former employee gatherings. The celebration culminated with Pattie Hyde Barclay cutting the 50th Anniversary cake at the membership banquet.

At the banquet Walter Ruesch presented his Managing Director's report. He announced that over $500,000 had been spent bringing facilities up to modern standards. While the Conference was forging into the future he reminded those in attendance that:

> ...our purpose remains the same as (it was) fifty years ago - to serve conferences of a religious and educational nature, to serve families in a family camping program in a Christian atmosphere, and to serve our staff of college students by giving them work experience....

He closed stating that the main thrust of the Association would be to develop winter programs for families and conferences.

Pattie Hyde Barclay cuts the 50th Anniversary cake.
Lula W. Dorsey Museum   Carl Larson

Fifty Cabins In Five Years

During the spring of 1960, while driving the winding two lane road that later became Interstate 25, Walter Ruesch had an idea that forever changed the character of the YMCA of the Rockies. The drive had provided Ruesch with lots of "windshield time" to think. By the time he arrived back in Estes Park, Ruesch had formulated a plan to build 50 new cabins in three years. To finance the program, patrons would contribute the necessary funds or place money in a prepaid rent account. In return they received first priority in making reservations for a specific period of time.

Henry Dorsey Jr. became excited about the program and offered to build several cabins for the Association. Not being content with merely writing a check, he wanted to personally pick cabin sites. With the cabin dimensions in hand and a carload of stakes, Dorsey and Louis Moore walked the side of Emerald Mountain during the summer of 1960. When they found a likely spot, Dorsey framed the view of the mountains with his hands like a movie director marking the spot for the living room window. Louis Moore ran a line parallel to Dorsey's out-stretched hands to mark off the front corners of the cabin.

Ruesch's plan found favor not only with the Dorseys but others as well. At the November 1960 Board meeting it was reported that 15 cabins were under construction with foundations laid for 17 more. By again purchasing supplies in carload lots and building cabins in an assembly line fashion the price was held to $8,000 each. Three years later Ruesch reported that 37 of the 50 cabins were complete with six more under construction. Although it took an additional two years to complete all 50, the project was a resounding success.

Building cabins assembly line fashion.
Lula W. Dorsey Museum

Politics of the Cold War

The YMCA had always held itself out as a bastion of stability; however, the politics of the 1960s were too strong to hold back.

John T. Clingan, District Director of the U.S. Department of Justice appeared before the Board during the Cuban Missile Crisis. He expressed the Government's interest in renting the grounds to house enemy aliens and foreign diplomats during national emergencies. Clingan indicated that "until the enemy is identified they (are) working only on an estimate of the number of people this would involve, but there are 38,000 aliens in Colorado, Wyoming, and Utah." They would be rounded up by the FBI and interred until deported or given the all clear by the President. The Government also requested office space for the Attorney General, U.S. Marshals, Customs, and Immigration and Naturalization Service. The Board passed a resolution making the grounds available in an emergency.

Three years later, in May 1965, politics of the Cold War era again made its presence felt when a new program aimed at educating staff and guests about the dangers of Communism was unveiled. Program Director Edward J. Rohmann, said "the most important problem confronting our country is that of communism." He further justified the new program by stating "the lack of knowledge, degree of misinformation, and subtle effects of communistic penetration among liberal movements and colleges are self evident."

The program resulted in the largest attendance by student employees and guests in years. The two speakers, one of whom cited 25 year old information and the other who could not back up his claims, were ill prepared. They not only inflamed liberal college students, but offended factions who thought that the subject of communism should not even be discussed at the YMCA of the Rockies. Management was deluged with both complaints and compliments.

The Longhouse

Providing meeting space for growing conference groups prompted one of the most memorable events of the Ruesch years. In 1959 Ruesch signed up 2800 Church of the Brethren youth for August 1962 with the stipulation that they would meet under one roof. The YMCA had no such facility, but that did not matter to Ruesch. He hurriedly located a circus tent in Fremont, Nebraska and made arrangements to rent it for the week.

During the fall of 1961 Ruesch visited Henry Dorsey Jr. in Dallas, Texas and, during the course of a conversation, Ruesch related the difficulties involved in housing the group's meetings. Dorsey took Ruesch to a large skating rink that was constructed from prestressed concrete and steel. Ruesch took one look at it and said it looked great, but the YMCA did not have one.

Dorsey decided that the YMCA should have such a building, and he was going to make it happen. Ruesch contacted President of the Board Dwight Dannen who gave a verbal okay on the project. On May 29, 1962 architect and Board member Ken Clark received a telephone call from Ruesch who tracked him down in Ogallala, Nebraska where he was working on a project. Ruesch told Clark he needed him in Estes Park "now." Clark drove to his home in Lincoln, hurriedly packed, and arrived in Estes Park the next day.

Board members and friends gather at the site of the Longhouse.
Lula W. Dorsey Museum

Dorsey, Ruesch, and Clark met on the hillside behind Hyde Memorial. Clark took some quick measurements and sightings and returned to Nebraska to engineer the foundation and prestressed concrete floors. Dorsey worked with the steel contractor in Dallas. After inspecting the final plans, Dorsey decided that the building was not big enough and made some changes. Clark quickly changed the engineering to match. When the steel arrived from Texas, the trucks could not make the turn into the grounds and the old rock pillars at the entrance were knocked down. Henry Dorsey set up a "command post" on the site where he oversaw the project.

When the Board of Directors arrived for their meeting in July they were greeted by the steel framework of the enormous Longhouse. Many had known that a building was under construction, but Ruesch failed to inform them of the magnitude of the project. Ruesch later remembered that he really took some heat for not keeping the Board informed!

As the first of August approached, the building was nowhere near completion. Construction crews started working 24 hours a day, 7 days a week. The day before the Brethren youth were due to use the building, the roof over the temporary stage was unfinished and the wiring was incomplete; however, the next night all 2800 were housed under one roof. Years later Ken Clark recalled that not since the days of World War II had he seen such a large building designed and completed in such a short period of time.

Family Programming Matures

The expansion of the Program Department and proliferation of activities begun in the 1940s under Ben Timmerman continued during Ruesch's administration. Program Director Ned Linegar recalled that with accommodations in substandard condition in the early 1950s, programming was extremely important. He said that, "if we could get them out of their cabins and into Program, then we knew we had 'em."

In the late 1940s, Program Department activities were housed in whatever space could be found. The Program information desk was located in the overcrowded Administration Building. Books on loan from the Colorado State Library were scattered about: books for adults were located in the Administration Building lobby, juvenile books in the Gopher Hole, and children's books in Kindernook. The Craft Shop was located under the Dining Hall along with the Art Studio. The Teenage Club was housed under the Assembly Hall. Table games were played in the Administration Building lobby and shuffleboard on the porch.

Guests read the Program bulletin board in the Administration Building.
Lula W. Dorsey Museum   F.P. Clatworthy Jr.

The post war baby boom made children's activities a major growth area for the Program Department in the 1950s. With attendance at Day Camp growing by leaps and bounds, a special facility was needed. Friendship House with its large common room was suited for that purpose. When it became overcrowded tepees housed the overflow. The tepees added to the western ambiance, but proved unsuitable during inclement weather.

In 1955 Jeep Gaston, Assistant Program Director in charge of Youth Programs, laid the foundation for modern youth programming at the YMCA of the Rockies. Children were divided into categories with activities suited to each age group. The Kindernook program was renamed Koral Kamp to disassociate it with connotations of kindergarten. In Koral Kamp, group play activities were stressed. Children who had finished the first grade were enrolled in Buckaroos. Activities included short hikes, nature study, cookouts, horseback riding in the riding ring, crafts, games, and singing.

Day Camp was geared to youth in the 2nd through 6th grades. Campers participated in trail rides, long hikes, nature study, crafts, miniature golf, art, archery, ping pong, riflery, square dancing, cookouts, camping trips, and games. Pioneer Camp included grades 7 through 9. Group planned activities were emphasized including camping, cookouts, all day hikes, long horseback rides, and sports. The Teenage Club provided activities for high schoolers. Again, group cooperation in planning activities such as parties, campouts, dances, hikes, and horseback rides was emphasized.

Since the first conference in 1908, hiking had been an important activity. During the 1950s, the hiking program reflected a renewed interest in hiking that was more than just destination oriented. Following the example of Enos Mills who pioneered guided nature hikes at the turn of the century, hikes at the YMCA were developed just to study plants and birds. By 1963 the hiking program had gained such popularity that a Volunteer Hikemaster program was started requiring candidates to pass a written and practical test before leading hikes.

With the Program Department bursting at the seams, management and Board began looking for ways to solve the problem. A Board subcommittee suggested building a craft shop between the Assembly Hall and the Administration Building turning the current Post Office/Grocery Store into a teenage center. Later, a master plan was submitted that would turn that building into an Art Studio and Craft Shop, but upon further study, it was decided to move Program activities outside the core area because of congestion.

Walter G. Ruesch, 1952.
Lula W. Dorsey Museum

The YMCA livery, now the Teen Barn.
Lula W. Dorsey Museum

Story time at Day Camp.
Lula W. Dorsey Museum   F.P. Clatworthy Jr.

Cookouts eased the burden on over crowded dining facilities.
Lula W. Dorsey Museum

The Craft Shop under the Walnut Room.
Lula W. Dorsey Museum

Al Wands gives an art lesson.
Lula W. Dorsey Museum

In 1954 Ruesch submitted a plan to build a 2,400 square foot building to house all Program activities including Day Camp. The plans were scaled down somewhat and Dick Hall was finished in 1955. Dedicated in honor of past President of the Board Lewis A. Dick, it provided much needed relief for the Program Department. Dick Hall was used for square dancing, movies, plays, talent shows, and some Day Camp activities, but it was far from adequate to house all Program activities.

While programming was a big growth area in numbers of guests served, it had a negative impact on the bottom line of the Association. Staff devoted to programming had increased from 11 in 1948 to 44 in a short time. Ruesch addressed the problem stating, "the cost of Program has increased considerably, and we need to decide whether we need to continue developing new programs and put in more money... or hold the line." While it was recognized that certain areas of Program such as crafts made money, most did not. The Board quickly decided that with the Association turning more and more into a family resort, expansion of Program activities was a necessity.

The result of the Board's decision to continue expanding the Program Department became readily evident. In 1958 Ned Linegar was named Associate Director in charge of Program. One of his primary responsibilities was to develop winter programs. In 1957 the old ice house was remodeled into a warming hut for ice skaters, and a toboggan run was built.

On August 23, 1959 the Jellison Youth Building was dedicated through the generosity of Mr. and Mrs. A.D. Jellison. It gave the Day Camp adequate space for the first time. In 1960 the Program Department moved into its own building, Sweet Memorial. Finally, management of Program's over 100 activities was consolidated under one roof. Sweet Memorial also served as the winter office for the Conference since the Administration Building was not yet winterized. Despite a decade of planning, the Craft Shop was still in cramped quarters underneath the Dining Hall. It was finally moved into "temporary" quarters underneath the Longhouse.

Since the early 1950s, the YMCA livery operation had grown by leaps and bounds. Management had found that owning its own string of horses was more trouble than it was worth. The horses had to be taken to the lowlands every fall and returned in the spring. Tack had to be maintained and horses kept healthy.

In 1962 the YMCA got out of the livery business when Bill Robinson obtained a concession to operate the livery. As a teenager he had worked for Art Card who owned several liveries in Estes Park including the Fall River Lodge livery in Horseshoe Park. Robinson bought that livery from Art in 1954 and owned it until 1959. From 1959 to 1962 he owned the Steads Ranch livery.

A decision was made to relocate the livery from its location in the draw north of the Second Mesa to west of Friendship Lodge. The old location was cramped, had inadequate pasture, and the odor offended nearby guests. Originally, the old livery built in 1922 was scheduled to be leveled, but Ruesch decided to convert it to a teenage recreation center, the Teen Barn. "The Barn" provided a place the teens called their own. There they gathered to enjoy music, dance, and just hang out.

While Jellison provided a facility for older youth, younger children were still packed into the old Wyoming building housing Kindernook. In 1965 Mr. Richard E. Bennett gave Koral Kamp it own modern facility when he made possible Bennett Children's Building.

On July 26, 1964, the Jellison Library, also made possible through the generosity of Mr. and Mrs. A.D. Jellison, was dedicated. No longer were reading materials scattered about in various places. However, the library did not just one day open its doors for business. It personified the dedication and "can do" attitude of Ruesch's seasonal staff.

With nothing but a blueprint and a planned ground breaking, Walter Ruesch and Elmer Magee went to Lincoln, Nebraska to visit with Gwendoline Birky, a librarian in the Lincoln Public Schools. She accepted their invitation to help open a library. Arriving in June 1963 she was surprised to find only a hole in the ground.

With her experience, Birky was allowed to act as consultant regarding the interior layout and equipment needed to make the library functional. Architects had failed to provide the necessary workroom or plan for slanted reading tables for children. With no library, she worked in the gift shop by day and cataloged the small collection of books located in Sweet Memorial by night.

To ascertain the composition of the library's collection, questionnaires were mailed to regular guests, Board members and employees. The final tabulation indicated a need for children's literature, adult fiction, books on religion, Colorado history, ghost towns, mining and the flora and fauna of the region.

On Birky's last day at work she and Ellen Baker drove to Denver to second hand bookstores on a buying expedition. Mr. Ruesch had given them several hundred dollars to spend. At the first store, they inquired if the owner would consider allowing a discount for such a worthy cause. They were given a 20% discount. Fortified with success they visited two additional shops and were equally successful. Thus, they ended up with a carload of books for much less than anticipated.

The next summer Mary Capps, Gwendoline Birky, and a guest volunteer began cataloging and processing the books. As the building was without furniture, they worked on the carpeted floor of the main room. Since the Colorado Library Commission had again lent the YMCA a large collection, the Jellison Library was able to open in July 1964 with a good selection of books.

Since the founding of the Western Conference, construction of a swimming pool was a goal of many Executive Secretaries, Managing Directors, and Board Members. When a master plan which included a pool was submitted in 1955, it was evident that there was not unanimous agreement on the subject. Some felt that a "swimming pool was out of character in a mountain setting and costly to maintain." Others felt just as strongly "that there is a real need for one to completely round out the recreational program."

In 1956 the Board authorized construction of a pool as soon as funds were available. In 1959 Ruesch conducted a spot survey of guests and found that 100% said they would use a pool if available. The Program Committee appointed a subcommittee to study size, design, and cost.

It was not until May 1964 that it was announced that substantial contributions toward construction of a pool had been received from the Dwight Dannen and Charles Mannschreck families as well as Lula Dorsey in memory of her brother Henry Dorsey Jr. When the Henry Dorsey Jr. Memorial Pool was dedicated on July 31, 1966 it fulfilled a 56 year dream.

Calling the square at the annual Square and Folk Dance Festival.
Lula W. Dorsey Museum

The newly completed Jellison Library.
Lula W. Dorsey Museum

A dream come true, the Henry Dorsey Jr. Memorial Swimming Pool.
Lula W. Dorsey Museum

Seasonal Staff's Golden Age

The growth of the Estes Park Conference after World War II brought to the forefront the need for a large stable work force. Securing seasonal staff during the early days was not a problem since the grounds were open only during the summer. The professional and managerial staff were borrowed from Denver or other YMCAs. Other key staff were affiliated with colleges or universities which left their summers open for work at Estes Park. Other positions were filled by children of staff, local residents, college students who previously attended a conference, or by word of mouth.

There was no active recruitment program for seasonal staff until 1938 when Secretary A.L. Mayer made contacts with college Student YMCAs and local Associations concerning supplying the Conference with seasonal employees. In 1939 the Estes Park Conference made serving seasonal staff part of its mission by sponsoring seminars aimed at helping students assume positions of responsibility or improve existing leadership skills in student YMCAs and YWCAs.

The importance of seasonal staff to the Association was emphasized by the construction of the Mummy Quadrangle and Employee Recreation Hall in the late 1940s. Ben Timmerman continued Mayer's emphasis on the spiritual and intellectual needs of the seasonal staff by expanding The YMCA - YWCA Leadership Training Seminar.

Organized by Hal Kuebler, the employee Seminar was held for six weeks during the middle of the summer. It was expressly designed to help students assume positions of leadership in their Campus Christian Associations. Seminar topics included Racial Misunderstanding, Economic Injustice, and International Tension. Field trips to social agencies in the Denver area were also part of the scheduled program.

The normal work week consisted of eight hours per day six days per week. The pay was $1 per day including room and board; students who stayed through Labor Day received a bonus of $10, and an additional $30 from the Appreciation Fund. In 1956 the pay was increased to $2 per day.

The growth of the Estes Conference during the 1950s and early 1960s necessitated proportional growth in the number of seasonal staff. In 1955 the seasonal staff numbered 200; by 1964 it stood at 300. The summer staff of the early 1950s was nearly 75% female, primarily from the midwest and southwest. Not all were students, about 20% were senior staff. The staff was a closely knit group. Few had cars, so the Conference organized activities for staff "en masse." All aspects of student life were closely monitored by Helen Matthews, staff counselor.

Even though the work week was 48 hours there was time for many social events organized through the Employee Association. There were Saturday night parties, trips to Cheyenne Frontier Days, concerts at Red Rocks, Employee Carnivals, vespers, Cross and Communion services, and operas at Central City. The staff produced elaborate plays and dramatic presentations. The Employee Association was also charged with the responsibility for disciplining employees running afoul of the rules.

Two of the most enduring activities involving staff are Christmas in July and the 4th of July parade. Christmas in July was first celebrated in 1912 when students, teachers, their families, and employees gathered in the Administration Building. For seasonal employees away from their homes and families, their co-workers became an extended family. All of the activities normally associated with Christmas are enjoyed, including exchange of presents, trimming trees, caroling, and religious services.

The 4th of July has been celebrated at the YMCA of the Rockies since 1911. The highlight of the Independence Day celebration is a festive parade participated in by all departments. "Floats" are made from whatever vehicles and materials available. The celebration is punctuated by youthful exuberance and creativity. Even summer thunderstorms never dampen the festive atmosphere.

Until the late 1950s the Student Seminar was still an important part of the employee program since most staffers were usually involved in YMCA-YWCA or other religious activities on campus. However, by 1958 the Seminar was beginning to decline in importance since only one-third of the staff was affiliated with the college YMCA-YWCA movement.

The mass social unrest of society and its youth that occurred in the 1960s along with the demise of the college YMCA-YWCA greatly affected the Estes Park Conference staff. No longer were they an almost homogeneous group but reflected the diversity of a changing society.

George Katibah and the ice truck, "Betsy."
Lula W. Dorsey Museum

Staff takes a break for the annual 4th of July parade.
Lula W. Dorsey Museum

Staffers board the "Gold Bug" to go hiking.
Lula W. Dorsey Museum

Conferences Compete For Space

During the late 1950s and early 1960s, the Estes Park Conference was dealing with an identity crisis. Was the YMCA a family resort or a conference center? When the Summer School failed and conference business dropped off during the Depression, family utilization of the grounds was the mainstay of the Association. Some family vacationers resented invasion of "their Y camp" by ever growing conference groups.

While the Association continued to remain family oriented in its programming during the 1950s, it continued to rely more and more upon the revenues of conference groups for capital expenditures. In 1951 the Conference served a total of 50 groups. Ten years later the Association hosted 160 groups in the off season alone!

Not only was the number of groups growing, but their size grew as well. In 1956 the Conference hosted 1,400 men for the International YMCA Men's Conference, 1,200 of whom stayed on grounds. Facilities were stretched to the limit.

Ruesch later joked about the ingenuity required to serve large groups in the 1950s. Meeting rooms were packed with bunk beds which had to be dismantled and reassembled every day. Even the lumber warehouse was sometimes bunked. Conference groups laughingly called it "Lumber Inn." By 1962 the picture had changed radically. Groups of 1000 previously considered unwieldy were handled with ease. In 1962 when 2000 Church of the Brethren youth descended on the Conference, they were not only housed and fed but were also taken on hikes by the Program Department.

By 1964 group business had become so important to the Association that Garland Matthews was hired as Conference Coordinator on a year round basis. His primary responsibility was to see to the needs of groups while on the grounds. Matthews visited every group at its first meal welcoming them to the YMCA and answering any questions they might have.

Problems with Success

The official records of the Estes Park Conference are filled with glowing reports of increased business and revenue, but there were dips along the way. Ruesch learned early in his tenure that doing business with conference groups could be frustrating. In 1952 he complained that group business was drastically down despite marketing efforts. Problems with guaranteeing group numbers continued. In 1960 several large groups canceled at the last minute. With the budget in place, seasonal staff hired, and capital expenditures underway, expenses went way over budget.

Ruesch's solution to the sometimes fickle conference business was to suggest increasing marketing efforts. As he indicated to the Board in 1962, "we've got all we can handle in peak summer." Early June was still a slow period, and of course, marketing was needed to fill new winterized accommodations.

Winterization of facilities was intended to increase revenues on a year-round basis and to provide additional funds for capital expenditures. In both respects it was highly successful, but again there were problems. Board and Management found out that increased business resulted in increased overhead. Additional operating expenses in the areas of staffing, insurance, and utilities were especially troublesome. In 1956 Ruesch complained that obtaining staff and housing them for winter operations was difficult.

Nature provided its own roadblocks to successful winter operations. In January 1963 Program Director Edward Rohmann lamented that a lack of snow forced Hidden Valley Ski area to remain closed until mid January. Five out of the ten youth groups scheduled to stay on the grounds during Christmas canceled.

The growth of Conference operations during the 1950s, both in numbers of guests served and in expanded operations, was not without its opponents. Some guests, staff, and Board expressed concern over the Conference growing at such a dizzying pace thus losing its small camp atmosphere. The Reservations Office was turning 25 families down for every one accommodated. Ruesch met such criticism head on stating that people wanting to keep things status quo were "selfish."

Lois and Ed Hill back from a morning drive in their new Pontiac.
Lula W. Dorsey Museum   Fred P. Clatworthy Jr.

Going Home To Grand County

During the summer of 1964, Walter Ruesch was contacted by a young preacher wanting to start an operation similar to the Estes Park Conference in Cripple Creek, Colorado. When Ruesch presented the proposal to the Board of Directors it was met with a mostly positive response. Board member Jim Eggleston cautioned not to move too boldly without adequate planning. Paul Hayward said the YMCA should think in terms of improving service to its present constituency. It was pointed out that Estes Park was reaching saturation with the demand for accommodations far exceeding supply. Besides, as Ruesch later remembered, "the proposition sounded interesting."

The Search

Board members Dwight Dannen and Wendel Ley along with Ruesch were appointed to investigate the proposition. They visited Cripple Creek several times looking for suitable locations. They found one, but the parcel's nearly 200 owners including mineral claimants were scattered all over the world. Clearing up questions of ownership would require expensive legal work. When a flash flood wiped out the water system serving the land, a decision was made to look elsewhere.

Singing River Ranch owned by the Denver YMCA was another possibility. Dwight Dannen went to Colorado Springs in May 1965 to inspect the ranch. After reporting his findings, Singing River Ranch was marked off the list as well. In spite of two disappointments the Executive Committee authorized purchase of land as soon as a suitable location was found.

At the July 1965 Board meeting, Wendel Ley said the YMCA should hasten its search for additional land because growth in the skiing industry would soon deplete desirable land. His fellow Board members agreed, developing a list of prerequisites. They reasoned that 1500 to 2000 acres with National Forest land nearby for recreational use was required. There must be a mountain suitable for skiing, with five to six feet of natural snow or sufficient water rights to make snow. Additional requirements included level land for buildings, plenty of open space, and good tree cover. The Board realized that easy accessibility and good transportation were important as well.

Six months of travel, correspondence, discussion, inspection, mountain climbing, and map reading led to the discarding of all sites in Colorado, beautiful as they were, except for those within a one hundred mile radius west of Denver.

On November 18, 1965 Dwight and Mary Ellen Dannen arrived in Denver at 9:40 a.m. on Continental Airlines. There they met Wendel and Audrey Ley and Walter Ruesch. The purpose of their trip was to inspect a 1,200 acre ranch in the Gore Range that sounded as if it might satisfy the prerequisites. Although the ranch was small, it bordered the Blue River and Forest Service land useful for program activities.

Almost as an afterthought, Ruesch handed them a brief note on something called the Just Ranch. Jack Orr of Van Schaack Realty had passed the information to Ruesch only that morning. The couples wanted to spend the night in Vail and time was limited. Maps indicated that a short detour through Tabernash to visit the Just Ranch would still enable them to see the Blue River property before dark.

Following lunch at Fraser, they drove to Granby. Missing the turn to the Just ranch, they made a u-turn only after some serious consideration whether it was worth the effort. A blanket of fresh snow made the crown of the road barely discernable from the ditch. They made their way through the Acord ranch. The fresh snow made old wagons, machinery, and even the trash in the yard look attractive. Under the blanket of snow every tree reminded them of Christmas.

Making their way towards the Just ranch they unknowingly passed a hurrying pickup truck containing Rudy Just and his wife, Clarabelle. They proceeded down the tree lined road to the ranch. Its log buildings looked enchanting under the blanket of snow. The house was tucked below the brow of the hill overlooking Pole Creek. Beyond rose Sheep Mountain and off to the right up the valley lay the Blue Ridge. Della Just, the owner, ushered them into her living room. From above the antlers on the wall, she took a map showing the ranch. From it they were able to visualize its boundaries.

The Just ranch homestead.
Lula W. Dorsey Museum   Jack Melton

Seeing their stop at the Just ranch as a diversion to their true goal, the couples headed on to Kremmling to the confluence of the Colorado and Blue Rivers. Dwight Dannen remembered "the rancher, in Texas style, owned everything he could see, but unfortunately, he couldn't see far enough." Although beautiful, the tract was too small, the price too high, and land too steep.

After visiting Kremmling, their thoughts returned to the Just Ranch. Its potential excited them. With 14 inches of snow already on the ground there was little time left before winter's heavy snows blanketed everything. In December, Ley and Ruesch made a two day inspection of the ranch. In a Jeep furnished by Van Schaack Realty they drove up Blue Ridge where they could see Pole Creek, the Fraser River, Granby, the Arapaho Mountains, and the west side of Rocky Mountain National Park including Longs Peak and the Never Summer Range. Ley remembered that "contrary to Henry Kaiser's advertising, the jeep could not go everywhere; we became high-centered in the deep snow along the meadows."

The next day, they rented a snowmobile to go where the jeep could not. This led to many adventures with "greenhorns" driving a snowmobile for the first time. Everything they saw was beautiful, and their verdict was "purchase." The go ahead to begin negotiations with the Just family was received via telephone from President of the Board, Dwight Dannen. During early spring, Ruesch again visited the ranch and returned with favorable comments. His only negative observation was that, "there is a great deal of trash, treetops, and stumps on the property which some day must be cleaned up."

Dwight Dannen, Kent Dannen, and Wendel Ley visited the Ranch in July before the Board meeting. Seeing the Just ranch for the first time in summer, they were delighted with its beauty. In a rented car they ventured onto steep, narrow logging roads. Many meadows, hills and valleys on the ranch were given tentative names by the trio.

Later that month during the annual Board meeting, members and their wives made one final inspection of the property. Caravaning over on July 24, they picnicked in Piano Meadow. Dwight Dannen remembered that:

> Lem Jones, overcome by the spirit of discovery, passed the Piano Meadow turn-off, driving as far as the trail would take him up Blue Ridge.... When found, at the head of Pole Creek, he insisted he was not lost, but was merely staking his claim for a cabin site.

Elmer Magee caught the first fish out of Pole Creek for the YMCA. After lunch, the group drove to the ranch house. While the wives visited with Della and Clarabelle Just, the men inspected the array of machinery that cluttered the yard including rusting vehicles and a sawmill.

They also explored the Rowley homestead. In the cabin was an old wood stove in surprisingly good condition. In the house and barns were stacks of magazines and newspapers dated 1943. In the barn, bridles and parts of harnesses hung on the walls. The skeleton of an eagle was nailed to the outside wall of the log barn. Old saw mill equipment was in the yard, together with a homemade crane for lifting logs to the sawmill cradle. Even, the engine which furnished power was still there.

Parts of four large wagon wheels and a complete wagon of early manufacture were gradually falling apart In the front yard. An early Ford pick-up truck with running boards was also rusting away.

Approximately one hundred yards to the northeast of the Rowley House was a log cabin containing an old bed and rustic table. Against one side of the house out in the open, leaned an old piano - hence, the christening, "Old Piano Meadow." In the aspen trees nearby were two very old, rusted wood stoves.

At some point during the afternoon, the men gathered near the barn to hear Wendel Ley talk about the development potential of the ranch. Then he said:

> I believe we have a quorum here gentlemen, perhaps we should take a preliminary vote to see where all of us stand. All those in favor of purchasing the Just ranch and holdings will respond by saying "Aye."

The vote was unanimous. When the Board reconvened in Estes Park, William E. Sweet Jr. moved that the Estes Park Conference purchase the Just ranch for $115 per acres plus attorneys' fees.

Board members, staff, and families inspect the Just ranch.
Lula W. Dorsey Museum

The accumulated junk from years of ranching at the Just homestead.
YMCA of the Rockies

An old wagon gradually succumbs to gravity.
YMCA of the Rockies

The Two Faces of Middle Park

Snow Mountain Ranch is located at the southern end of a geographical area known as Middle Park. Its arbitrary boundaries are the Indian Peaks in the east, Berthoud Pass in the south, Gore Range in the west, and the Rabbit Ears Range in the north. Middle Park's elevation varies from 7,000 to 13,500 feet. Today's recreational skiers who fail to venture north of Winter Park and Mary Jane's ski slopes, gets a false impression of Middle Park. They fail to see the other face of the Park with its legacy of mining, homesteading, and ranching.

Snapshot of Middle Park History

The first visitors to Middle Park were Paleo-Indians. Summering there possibly as early as 7,800 BC, they hunted the abundant game. During the modern era, Ute and Arapaho Indians inhabited Middle Park. Like their predecessors they were summer residents who moved to the plains during the long winters which saw temperatures drop as low as 50 below zero in Middle Park.

There are similarities between Middle Park and Estes Park during the early exploration period. The first Anglo visitors were French fur trappers working the Park during the 1820s. In 1839 a ragtag group of filibusters, bent on taking control of the British Northwest, passed through Middle Park and thus became its first documented Anglo visitors. Rufus B. Sage who visited Estes Park camped in Middle Park during the summer of 1842. John C. Fremont mapped the Park during his 1844 expedition.

While the Earl of Dunraven never made it to Middle Park, the area did have its own visitor of English nobility. Sir George Gore visited Middle Park on a legendary hunting trip from 1854 to 1857. His entourage included several dozen men and numerous wagons transporting such amenities as vintage wine. Ranging from Colorado Springs to the lower Yellowstone, his slaughter of game included thousands of bison, many grizzly bears, and countless elk, antelope, and deer. Gore's visit to Middle Park was brief, and he never returned. His only legacy is the various places bearing his name.

About the time the fur trade died out during the 1850s, Middle Park got its first settlers. With the gold rush came an influx of humanity combing Middle Park looking for mineral wealth. They found only enough to make them keep looking. The only ones who made any real money in Middle Park were the land speculators. Settlement of Middle Park was hindered by its inaccessibility until Berthoud Pass was discovered in 1860.

With accessibility came Middle Park's first tourists. In 1863 William N. Byers, editor of the Rocky Mountain News, visited Middle Park and traveled to what is today Hot Sulphur Springs. Native Americans had long used the hot springs for medicinal purposes. To Byers, it was an opportunity to cash in on the tourist trade. He acquired surrounding land through methods which, while not illegal, were certainly questionable. In Hot Sulphur Springs he envisioned building a giant resort to which he would bring people from Denver. He met with modest success, because in August 1874 there were 200 to 300 tourists in Middle Park most of whom were headed for Hot Sulphur Springs.

Middle Park found its true identity in ranching during the last quarter of the nineteenth century. The Homestead Act which was supposed to open up western land to settlement actually proved a hindrance to Middle Park. Under the Act a man homesteaded 160 acres which had to be "proved up" by living on and working the land. More land could be added through what was called "additionals." Even with additionals ranches were too small to support a family in the context of western ranching. By the mid 1870s many of the smaller homesteads were being consolidated into large ranches as frustrated settlers "threw in the towel."

Life on Middle Park's ranches was an isolated existence. During the winter when snow often lay six feet on the level, visitors, except for the closest neighbors, were a rare occurrence. During major storms, windows had to be shoveled out to let light into cabins. Ranchers were often totally isolated for weeks on end. Schools were in session from April to November, because sending children into the elements was out of the question.

In 1874 the formal trappings of governmental organization came to Middle Park when Grand County was organized. With no mineral wealth and a sparsely inhabited county, services were severely limited by an inadequate tax base. Nevertheless, Grand County started to boom. Plats for nonexistent towns were laid out along nonexistent railroads. It seemed that everyone was speculating on real estate, minerals, and ranch land. When the bottom fell out in the late 1880s because of to the uncertainties of ranching, lack of adequate transportation, and failure of mining, Grand County settled back to an isolated self sufficient ranching lifestyle.

The next boom came to Grand County in 1904 when the railroad reached Middle Park with completion of the Moffat Road over Rollins Pass. The railroad breathed life into old communities and gave birth to new ones. Ranchers reaped benefits through better access to markets for their products. The result was slow but steady growth after the turn of the century.

Early Hot Sulphur Springs.
Courtesy of Colorado State Historical Society #4989

The Cozens Ranch in Middle Park.
Courtesy of the Grand County Historical Society

The Justs

The Justs represented a small influx of Austrian ranching families making Middle Park their home. There is some confusion about exactly when Karl Just and his father arrived in Grand County. One source indicates that he camped there in 1879 or 1880 returning permanently in 1881 or 1882. Another source indicates that the Justs came to Grand County in 1885.

In 1895 Karl Just married a 16 year old German-American, Adelia (Della) Lehman. Her family reached Grand County via Rollins Pass in 1880 settling on the South Fork of the Colorado River (now under Lake Granby). On Pole Creek, Della and Karl Just purchased a small log cabin with a dirt roof and squatter's rights for $50. By 1899 they completed a log house just in time for the arrival of their first child, Henry. Seven more children were born, all delivered by Karl Just.

Della Just rakes hay on the Rowley ranch.
Grand County Historical Society

The family prospered through hard work and perseverance. The Justs developed their water rights by building a series of irrigation ditches. The lush meadow on Pole Creek provided grazing for cows and sheep as well as tons of surplus hay. The Justs systematically added to their holdings, and by the late 1920s their ranch was said to be the largest in the upper Fraser Valley. At one time they owned most of what is now Snow Mountain Ranch and Winter Park Highlands.

Rudy Just, the sixth child, was born in 1909. He spent all but six years of his life in Middle Park. Four of those years were spent in the Pacific during World War II where he earned three Bronze Stars and two were spent working on ranches in Montana. After the war Rudy returned to Grand County and went into business with his mother, raising cattle and sheep.

Fred Rowley at his homestead.
YMCA of the Rockies

During Rudy Just's wartime absence, his mother added to the family holdings by purchasing an adjoining homestead from Fred Rowley in 1943. Fred and Martha Rowley first settled in the Grand Lake area in 1919. They settled next to the Justs and lived in a tent. The Rowleys had three children, two girls and one boy. They had "squatters rights" until 1926 when they were granted a homestead patent.

Fred Rowley built a small log cabin in place of the tent. The front porch had a characteristic Western Stick style design in the gable above the door. There were a number of outbuildings including a large barn so situated that the sun shown through its entrance even on short winter days. Even though Fred Rowley picked his location well, he lacked water rights essential for a successful ranching. Most of the water was owned by those settling the area during the 1880s. Luckily for the Rowleys, the Justs had more than ample water rights and did not mind the Rowleys using some of their water from Pole Creek. The first few years were hard. Fred Rowley was not able to make a living off his homestead, so he worked at the railroad roundhouse to supplement his ranching income. Eventfully, the Rowleys sold out to Della Just because they just could not make ends meet.

Della Just always had a pot of coffee on the stove and time to sit and talk. Walter Ruesch remembered that she was "one of the most gracious people you would ever want to meet...." She loved to tell stories. One of her favorites was about a crazy miner living near them working his "gold mine." As she told the story, he had "been told by God" that there was gold in that place. The miner dug till he ran out of money. Then he worked on the railroad buying more beans and flour to dig again. The miner claimed to have a semi-tame porcupine living under the loose floor boards of the cabin that came out and danced when he played his harmonica!

In 1965 Rudy Just married Clarabelle Raley Hughes. She added her own color to the Just legacy blending her stories and humor with that of Rudy's family. Born in Indian Territory (Oklahoma) she was one quarter Cherokee. In 1911 her parents loaded up the family's nine children, farm equipment, animals, and belongings and joined an immigrant train. They settled south of Silt, Colorado near Rifle. Although she was only a little over 5 feet tall, she spent a lifetime of ranching, wrangling, trapping, and homesteading. Clarabelle was working on the Just ranch when Rudy proposed to her, because as he said, "she was too good a help to lose."

The Other Face of Middle Park

Skiing is almost as deeply rooted in Middle Park history as ranching. In 1883 jumping hills were built in Hot Sulphur Springs. Although most of the competitors were locals, it did produce the first "ski boom" in Grand County. During those early days, old timers looked at recreational skiers with disdain, because they saw skiing as a necessity. It provided access to trap lines or to the next ranch.

When the Moffat Tunnel was completed in 1927, it provided quick, easy access to the slopes from Denver. Skiers disembarked at the western terminus of the Tunnel, and after a day of skiing, they caught an east bound train for the return trip to Denver. During those early days, skiing was primarily limited to the Jim Creek and Mary Jane Creek drainages. In the late 1920s, Denverite Graeme McGowan began looking for a place to develop a ski area. He purchased some old buildings from the railroad at the West Portal of the Tunnel and opened Jim Creek Lodge. The Colorado Arlberg Club continued McGowan's development by building a clubhouse and accommodations.

In 1933 recreational skiing received a boost from the Forest Service which improved Mary Jane Trail. Skiing in those days was different from today. Skiers hiked all morning to reach the top of the mountain then skied down for lunch. Only the most hardy would attempt an afternoon run. Some women accompanied the all male Arlberg Club but were not accepted as members until 1938.

In 1938 the city of Denver was granted a permit to develop 6,400 acres in the West Portal area. The city raised $17,000 to build a rope tow. When the money was exhausted volunteers cut trees and cleared land for ski trails. The name "Winter Park" was first used in the Denver media in January 1939. Winter Park was officially opened a few days later. Even during the lean years of World War II some development continued. However, skiing was still primitive. Much of the area's equipment was "jerry rigged" using volunteer labor.

Early ski jumping competition at Hot Sulphur Springs.
Grand County Historical Society

Growth of Winter Park accelerated during the late 1940s and early 1950s. Many creature comforts were added. Improved lifts and more trails gave it a skier capacity of 1,600, the highest in Colorado. About the same time Winter Park began to groom its slopes. Old timers protested saying that they should not smooth out the moguls. They were what skiing was all about.

Numbers of skiers doubled almost every year requiring better facilities, improved lifts, and more trails. In 1962, Winter Park's first chair lift was installed signaling an end to T bars; however, the last T bar was not taken out of service until 1978.

The tremendous growth of the skiing industry throughout the 1970s and 1980s was reflected in expansion of Winter Park. The opening of Snow Mountain Ranch in 1969 coincided with the planning for Mary Jane Ski area which opened in 1976. In 1976, Winter Park installed snow making equipment. Luckily, it was operational in time for the drought of 1976-1977. Expansion continued in the 1980s with new lifts and the opening of Vasquez Ridge and the "Backside" of Mary Jane.

The intertwined legacy of recreational skiing and ranching in Middle Park provides a fertile heritage for Snow Mountain Ranch. The Board of Directors brought the YMCA to Middle Park seeking a place to establish a winter playground, but it was the western ranch atmosphere that captivated them.

The Bob Wood Tow at Winter Park.

Charles E. Grover

From Y Camp to
YMCA of the Rockies

Transforming the Just ranch into Snow Mountain Ranch required an enormous amount of work. The Board hired the firm of Harrison and Ripple, Site Planning Consultants, to develop a master plan. Original plans envisioned Snow Mountain Ranch accommodating 10,000 persons served by a staff of 700. Many proposals including a downhill ski area were considered during the preliminary stages. Board and staff were equally caught up in the exhilarating task of planning and opening a totally new facility.

Overcoming Skepticism

The natural skepticism of locals who could not believe that the YMCA was opening a conference and family facility for 10,000 people had to be overcome. When they heard the name "YMCA" they immediately thought of the Denver YMCA boy's camp north of Granby. Their reaction was, "why another YMCA camp?"

Ruesch found the Grand County Commissioners equally skeptical. Many were conservative ranchers and strictly anti-development. Their negativism arose in part from the fact that the YMCA was non-profit and might take land off the tax rolls. As the only one to handle public relations problems, Walter Ruesch spoke to the local Kiwanas and Rotary Clubs about the YMCA's plans.

Local merchants were also skeptical of the new development, and many were reluctant to extend credit. In typical western fashion the YMCA had to "prove up" on its land. It was almost two years after the YMCA purchased the ranch that a local merchant offered to extend credit.

The Conference Changes its Name

In November 1967 Dr. Urban Busiek made a motion to change the name of the Estes Park Conference of the Young Men's Christian Association to the YMCA of the Rockies. The motion was seconded by J. Clinton Hawkins and approved by the Board.

The Board was merely making something official that had been in common usage for years. As early as 1948 the name appeared in print. In the 1950s the nickname "YMCA of the Rockies" increasingly appeared in advertising.

The Association's identity crisis had become such a problem that Walter Ruesch brought the reservation's registrar before the Board. She indicated that the YMCA was "known as the Estes Park Conference YMCA, the YMCA of the Rockies, and an endless variety of distortions of these two names." The problem was further compounded by the fact that the Post Office was named "Association Camp."

The purchase of Snow Mountain Ranch had finally forced the Board to take action. The old name did not truly reflect the multi-facility status of the Association. There was also concern over problems related to reservations and marketing that would arise from using the name Estes Park Conference in reference to the Winter Park facility. Consequently, on August 4, 1968 the official Corporate name of the Association was changed to "YMCA of the Rockies."

Becoming an Independent YMCA

Even with a change in Corporate name the YMCA of the Rockies was still not independent of outside control. In 1969, the West Central Area and Southwest Area were replaced with the Mid-America and Southwest Regions which still elected 50% the of YMCA of the Rockies Board members.

In 1974 the Association took a significant step toward independence when the By-Laws were changed so that 36 members of the Board were elected by the incumbent members with the Executive Directors of the Mid-America and Southwest Regions serving as members. It was not until 1985 that the YMCA of the Rockies became totally independent of the Regions, thus breaking the ties established before World War II.

Paying the Piper

The scope of the Snow Mountain Ranch project became apparent when E. Wilson Germany reported that estimates of projects on the drawing board had already reached $930,000 excluding architect fees. The Board realized that funding from Estes Park's excess operating revenues was not sufficient to develop Snow Mountain Ranch. E. Ray Siler moved that a committee of five be appointed to plan a strategy for raising funds and promoting Snow Mountain Ranch. A professional fund raising company was initially hired but proved unsuccessful. The YMCA of the Rockies took over the job with Wendel Ley chairing the campaign.

In a solicitation letter sent to friends of the Conference in 1968, President Dwight Dannen asked them to join the "Pioneering 400" by contributing $1,000 or more to get Snow Mountain Ranch off the ground. In part it stated: "we all need to put our shoulders to the wheel.... The founders of the Estes Park Conference did it over 60 years ago; we need to do it now."

After reviewing capital needs, the Board increased its fund raising goal to $1,500,000 and announced a capital fund drive named "Stake-a-Claim." The concept of the campaign centered around patrons "purchasing" an acre of land of Snow Mountain Ranch for $300. The campaign provided much needed capital for development. The Board also conducted a "quiet" campaign to raise additional funds.

While various methods of fund raising for Snow Mountain Ranch proved moderately successful, the majority of funds needed for development came from borrowing and excess revenues generated by the Estes Park Center.

Breaking Ground

Work on Snow Mountain Ranch began in earnest during the Spring of 1968 when Ty Woodward and Don Hay were transferred from Estes Park to Snow Mountain Ranch. When they arrived, they were greeted with beautiful spring weather. However, nature provided several surprises in the form of heavy, wet snows that turned roads into a "sea of mud."

The Woodwards were welcomed by the Justs with their usual western hospitality. On Memorial Day not long after their arrival, the Woodwards went down to the ranch house to ask Rudy if he knew where they could fish. Rudy immediately dropped everything saying, "if you are too busy to go fishing, you are too busy." They caught a couple of skillets full of trout. That evening they had a fine banquet finished off with fresh rhubarb pie.

· In a letter to her family Fern Woodward depicts how primitive and isolated Snow Mountain Ranch was in the spring of 1968:

> This letter has been on my mind for some time, but there has been too much to do or, things looked too discouraging - like leaky water pipes and soaked carpet

and all sorts of things that can happen in establishing a home in a second hand mobile home.... All modern conveniences are working now except the water heater and we should have it soon. We get some TV with a low aerial. This morning the picture of the Today show came in with the sound of Captain Kangaroo!

Mail service is something you wouldn't believe in the USA. We have to go to a post office, and since there isn't much to go to Tabernash for, we chose Granby which puts about 14 miles on the speedometer a round trip. We haven't been getting the mail every day so if you have a urgent message for us you might try the phone. It is a party line with 8 or 10 phones. Otherwise try smoke signals.

The Woodwards did not mind the rugged conditions or hard work, because as Fern Woodward recalled, "Ty enjoys pioneering, and we (are) here starting from scratch."

In July 1968 Walter Ruesch reported to the Board that, "the crew is working on Snow Mountain Ranch, clearing the land, building roads, and cutting timber." What the Board heard was, of course, a sanitized version of the back breaking work that was going on.

For a while there was, according to Fern, more "destruction than construction." She recalls that on one particular day 13 old ranch buildings were knocked down and set on fire. Ty Woodward described the task facing his crew stating, "the side of the roads and the woods were full of downed trees and tree tops left by loggers. Along the roads and timber trails mature trees had been pushed over by bulldozers." He recalled that during that first summer there were three or four young men studying to be Episcopal ministers working on the ranch. One in particular had a horrible time learning how to "work" since he had never done physical labor. Occasionally, staff were sent over from Estes Park to help.

Collapsing buildings abounded on the property.
Lula W. Dorsey Museum

The work was as hard on equipment as it was men. The tree roots were mixed with sand and rock which quickly took the edge off a chain and sometimes the teeth. With as many as five saws working at once, keeping them operating was a difficult task. When one Remington saw quit working, they found that the aluminum piston had turned to ash from overheating!

Snags were not the only thing piled up around the ranch. On the Acord property the forests and fields were littered with all kinds of cast off machinery and household items. The rusting machinery was dozed up into a pile "10 feet high and as big as two house roofs" according to Woodward. There was also a multitude of wine bottles cast off by Rudy Just's brother. Fern Woodward gathered them up trying her best to find something useful to do with them but failed.

Adequate utilities were a major problem in developing the ranch. There was no natural gas available north of Granby so Ruesch negotiated with Public Service to extend their lines. One of the most pressing problems was telephone service. When the YMCA inquired about a business line they were told that they had to share an eight party line! By pressing the issue Snow Mountain Ranch got a private line and improved service for its neighbors as well.

During the summer of 1968 Ruesch organized caravans to introduce YMCA patrons to the potential of Snow Mountain Ranch. A big tent was pitched in Piano Meadow where they feasted on fried chicken, potato salad, and watermelons. The three Justs, Rudy, Clarabelle, and Della, entertained guests with stories of hunting, ranching, and homesteading.

Walter Ruesch did his best to entertain as well. Rudy Just had a pet rooster that had taken a liking to Ruesch. He liked to coax the rooster to sit on his shoulder and crow to the delight of guests. After the entertainment was over, Ruesch talked to those present about the YMCA's plans for developing the Just ranch. During July and August of 1968 several groups of 20 to 60 people were introduced to Snow Mountain Ranch.

The Board realized that for several years Snow Mountain Ranch was going to show a negative cash flow no matter what they did. Income in any form was welcome; therefore, the YMCA continued the Justs' haying operation rather than let the land lie fallow. In 1966 Walter Ruesch reported to President Dannen that the YMCA had "put up 400 tons of hay at $50 per ton" totaling $20,000!

By summer's end, construction began in earnest. That winter Ty Woodward remembered, "I got my first real understanding of deep snow." The snow was so deep and the roads so narrow that a dozer was required to carve out wide spots roads for cars to pass. Snowshoes were standard equipment on their trucks, because "if you got off the plowed road you had to have them." Every vehicle was equipped with chains, and still they got stuck. Even a veteran telephone repairman got his truck buried and had to be extracted by the Snow Mountain Ranch crew. There was a bright side to the frequent snows, because Fern Woodward recalled that it gave "the little animals, snowmobiles, and snowshoes, a clean sheet to make their tracks on."

Haying in the Pole Creek Meadow.
YMCA of the Rockies

Bob Ruesch

Heavy winter snows made work difficult.
YMCA of the Rockies

In November 1968 Ruesch reported to the Board that water wells had been drilled, electricity installed, the lodge and first floor of the Administration Building closed in, and camping sites cleared. By March he reported the heating system was installed, three cabins were under construction, and development of camp sites was going well.

In June 1969 Ruesch and the Board realized that there was no way Snow Mountain Ranch would open as scheduled in June. Although 40 of the rooms in the lodge were ready and 150 reservations taken, the opening had to be put off. With promotional materials already printed, press releases sent to 659 newspapers, and ads placed in travel trailer industry publications work went on a seven day a week schedule. Eager to have some cash flow before the end of summer, priority was given to finishing Pinewood Lodge, the Administration Building, kitchen, dining room, grocery store, craft shop, laundry, and livery.

The first seasonal employees arrived shortly after July 4. The group of five included Scott Zorno. He and a friend Bob Wennergren had tried to hire on in Estes Park but were refused as being too young; however, persistence paid off when Ruesch hired them for Snow Mountain Ranch.

When they got to Snow Mountain Ranch they were greeted by Don Hay and Ty Woodward who announced they had no heat, water, or lights in their living quarters. With the kitchen likewise unfinished they were treated to Ty Woodward's outdoor cooking in Piano Meadow. Scott vividly remembers the day they got heat in the lodge and much welcome hot water.

The female staff fared slightly better since they arrived a little later. The girls were housed in the basement of the unfinished lodge, sleeping in rough homemade bunk beds. With shower facilities in short supply the ladies washed their hair in the urinals of the unused men's bathroom! They managed to find other novel uses for bathroom fixtures by washing dishes in the bathtub of room 215 in Pinewood Lodge as the dishwasher had not yet arrived.

The Administration Building under construction.
YMCA of the Rockies

The barely finished Administration Building.
Lula W. Dorsey Museum

Even with work progressing at a hectic pace, staff took time out to gather around a color television with rabbit ears and a very fuzzy picture to watch the first moon landing. With the dedication only days away the staff also took time to decorate the lobby of the Administration Building for the first Christmas in July celebration.

On July 25, 1969 (Christmas Day in July) Snow Mountain Ranch was dedicated. The service was held in the unfinished Administration Building lobby. The picture windows had not yet arrived, and of course, it rained. The dedication was attended by many locals who came to see what all the hullabaloo was about. According to Ty Woodward they found it "unbelievable to see that set-up down in the middle of the woods!"

Although obviously unfinished, Snow Mountain Ranch was dedicated and ready for guests. Among its first guests was the J.T. Almon family from Evansville, Indiana. Fifteen year old J.T. Almon II accompanied his parents John and Ina on the two week trip. The elder Almon was scheduled to attend a seminar at the University in Boulder. Wanting to mix a little pleasure with business they decided to spend some time at the Estes Park Center before going to Boulder. Arriving in Estes the Almons found Estes Park and the YMCA packed with people at peak season.

Someone at the Estes Park Center told them about a new "camp" that was just opening on the other side of the mountains. Game for a little adventure, the family headed west over Trail Ridge with young Almon at the helm of the family's Buick Electra. They had a tough time locating SMR since it was marked with a small inconspicuous sign.

Arriving at the Administration Building they found everything in an "orderly state of chaos" with workmen scurrying about. They stayed in Pinewood Lodge along with a handful of other guests. At Snow Mountain Ranch the Almons found a friendly atmosphere reminiscent of a large family. Things were so informal that if guests were hungry they went to the kitchen, made a sandwich, and left an I.O.U. The informality continued at scheduled meal times. Young Almon remembered learning to fly fish and bringing his catch to the dining room to be prepared with eggs and toast for breakfast!

After two or three days, the Almons left for Boulder. Spending one day there, mother and son decided they had seen enough and headed back to Snow Mountain Ranch to wait for the senior Almon to complete his work. During the intervening three or four days, young Almon went riding exploring the woods, homesteads, and surrounding environs. Almon was befriended by a couple of the young men on staff who took him to Granby where he bought a pair of Justin boots which he still wears. After three or four days they drove back to Boulder, picked up the elder Almon and returned home.

Snow Mountain Ranch was open, even if somewhat prematurely. At the November 1969 Board meeting, Ruesch reported that the total revenues for Snow Mountain were only $36,000 resulting in a $13,000 operating loss. Ruesch praised the Board for its far sightedness in developing the Ranch and reminded them that additional facilities were necessary to bring Snow Mountain Ranch to a break even point.

Snow Mountain Ranch Grows Up

In November 1970 at its first meeting at Snow Mountain Ranch, the Board heard staff report on an urgent need for all types of facilities. Income producing projects were given priority as it was imperative that Snow Mountain Ranch produce sufficient income to amortize its own indebtedness.

During the first two years of operation there were only eight cabins available and demand out stripped supply several fold. Ruesch dealt with the problem in a novel way. In May 1971 twelve Red Dale camping trailers were purchased for $1,800 each. Flyers were sent to customers who were turned down for cabins telling them they could "enjoy the fun of living in a travel trailer without having to bring it with you." The trailers were booked from June 20 to Aug 22. To alleviate the cabin crunch, 41 cabins were built between 1969 and 1981.

In 1971 Whispering Pine Chapel was finished and Geronimo Campground opened. Two years later the Country Store was built. Staff urged construction of a building to be used for large groups and winter recreation such as basketball and volleyball. Consequently, credit left over from a previous construction loan was used to construct the Kiva Building in 1974.

Since conference groups provided the bulk of the Association's income, emphasis was given to building lodges. Aspenbrook and Silver Sage Lodges were opened in 1974 and Blue Ridge Lodge in 1976.

Programming Snow Mountain Ranch Style

During the first years of operation, the major hurdle faced by SMR Program staff was a lack of facilities. Hiking, fishing, and horseback riding were the most popular activities. The watchwords for programming were flexibility and adaptability. Day Camp and many other activities were operated out of the basement of the Administration Building. In 1976 Program finally received its own building freeing up valuable space in the Administration Building.

One of the first winter Program activities at Snow Mountain Ranch was snowmobiling. The snowmobile had provided both transportation and recreation at Snow Mountain Ranch since the initial explorations of Walter Ruesch and Wendel Ley in 1965. The spider web of logging roads made fine snowmobile trails. Under control of novices the machines were a maintenance nightmare and occasionally dangerous, but the large tracts of land at Snow Mountain Ranch made for great adventure.

Availability of downhill skiing was one of the primary considerations for purchasing the Just ranch. The Board initially envisioned developing its own ski area with beginning and intermediate slopes as well as a gondola lift. With capital requirements in the hundreds of thousands of dollars the project was deferred. Expansion of Winter Park and opening of Mary Jane combined with economic recession of the early 1980s finally spelled the death knell for the planned ski resort at Snow Mountain Ranch.

In 1971 a recommendation was made to add Nordic skiing to Program activities as an alternative until a ski hill was built. Nordic skiing was tried on an experimental basis in 1972. It was an instant success. The old logging roads made perfect Nordic trails. Soon, lessons and rental equipment were added which played a major role in shaping the future personality of Snow Mountain Ranch.

Nordic skiing immediately came into conflict with snowmobiles using the same trails. After evaluating the conflict, snowmobiles were relegated to certain trails under controlled conditions. By 1985 snowmobiles lost out all together, giving way to the swish of cross country skies.

Under an agreement with the YMCA, the Justs were given a lifetime lease on the ranch house and surrounding land. Their presence provided a unique programming opportunity for Snow Mountain Ranch. Clarabelle Just continued to trap for a living tanning the hides herself. She kept a trunk full of furs with which she put on programs. As she passed the furs among guests, Clarabelle Just told stories and tall tales of ranching, trapping, and hunting in Middle Park.

Early on, the Program Department learned two valuable lessons. First, people were not eager to participate in physical activities after a hard day of skiing. Recreation such as lectures, bridge, ski films, fireside songfests, and crafts were favored. Second, a winter youth program was one of the keys to success. It allowed parents to go skiing while the YMCA took care of the children.

Soon other activities shaped the Program personality at SMR. Program Director Barb Stemple reported that whitewater rafting was probably the largest growth area in program activities. Old fashioned sleigh rides also proved a hit with guests.

Snowmobiling provided entertainment for guests.
YMCA of the Rockies

Clarabelle and Rudy display their furs.
Lula W. Dorsey Museum

Ups and Downs

From an unsteady if not premature opening, Snow Mountain Ranch had only one direction to go and that was up. However, as with any business the curve was not always up.

Dick Engle, Resident Director, issued glowing reports to the Board stating that winter occupancy rates had nearly doubled during the period 1971-72. However, he soon learned that Spring or "mud season" was a dead period for Snow Mountain Ranch. There was not enough snow left to ski and too much mud to do anything else. In 1972 there was much excitement over the possibility of Colorado hosting the 1976 Olympics which would undoubtedly schedule some events in the vicinity of Winter Park. Unfortunately, the voters of the state were not as excited and voted down the proposal.

With tourist facilities in Colorado growing at a record pace, the YMCA of the Rockies found itself in a very competitive market. No longer could the Association sit back and wait for the telephone to ring. One problem faced by the Association was convincing the non-skiing public to drop its misconception that Snow Mountain Ranch was isolated and impossible to reach during the winter.

In 1973 Snow Mountain Ranch benefitted from its relative isolation by being selected to host a group of returning Vietnam Prisoners of War and their families. The quiet solitude gave families a place to get reacquainted and heal the psychological wounds of war.

The era of cheap oil that had fueled the world's economy came to an abrupt end in 1973 when the Organization of Petroleum Exporting Countries declared an oil embargo against the industrialized world. When shipments resumed the price of oil had quintupled.

The oil embargo's effect on Snow Mountain Ranch was immediate and dramatic. During Christmas many conference groups canceled or dropped dramatically in number as transportation costs skyrocketed. Four weeks of conferences including two groups of over 1,000 persons canceled during the height of the fuel shortage.

After Christmas, management realized that significant effort was required to keep the bottom line balanced. During late winter and early spring, potential guests in Colorado and surrounding states were targeted with marketing mailings. Use of the campgrounds was increased by a listing in the Woodall's Campground Directory. The marketing efforts paid off somewhat, but still Snow Mountain Ranch was left with an abundance of red ink.

The down turn in business was short lived, because at the November 1975 Board meeting it was proudly announced that Snow Mountain Ranch had shown sufficient income to amortize its own indebtedness. This was welcome news considering the operating deficits of previous years. Conference Coordinator Bob Ruesch reported that SMR "has come into its own." The staff took pride in reporting that 1,400 Evangelical Free Church youth were recently accommodated. That was some feat considering that the advertised capacity of Snow Mountain Ranch was about 1,100!

In July 1976 Dick Engle reported that operations were really starting to stabilize. Newly installed snow making equipment at Winter Park and the new Mary Jane ski area had combined for a great winter season in spite of a drought. In November 1976 it was reported that Snow Mountain Ranch grossed over $1,000,000 for the first time.

Meanwhile Back in Estes Park

While most of the YMCA of the Rockies resources were committed to Snow Mountain Ranch, work at the Estes Park Center did not come to a complete stop. The YMCA purchased and successfully developed a major addition to the property. In response to a changing society, corporate goals were defined, resulting in new facilities and program offerings. There were threats to stability by too little or too much moisture and a rebellious seasonal staff questioning established norms of behavior.

The YMCA Goes Shopping

In 1966 the YMCA of the Rockies made a land acquisition at the Estes Park Center that was minuscule compared to the Just ranch but very important to the Association. Many felt the main grounds of the Estes Park Center was nearing its maximum carrying capacity. Logically, the Board looked at available land near the Center. Several diverse properties were considered including acquiring the lease for the Estes Park Campground at the end of Tunnel Road and purchase of the Blue Arrow Campground. The land comprising the Park Lodge and Dunraven Inn was also considered. For various reasons they were all eliminated.

In 1965 the YMCA was approached by Bodie Smith who wished to sell 120 acres across Tunnel Road from the main grounds. Through negotiation a contract was signed one year later. With the excess revenue occupied with development of SMR, the land lay fallow for several years.

In 1970, Ruesch unveiled plans for the newly named Summit property envisioning a "development for mature people who would like to be removed from the busy main camp...." Original plans called for a small lodge, clusters of cabins, and a community center. Two years later the Board authorized an expenditure of $3,000 to plat the property. Construction began as soon as utilities were available.

In November 1973 Ruesch reported that the first two cabins were under construction; unfortunately, the foundations were not on YMCA owned land. When the land was purchased, the previous owners retained five acres on the most scenic part of the property on which they intended to build. Development came to a stop while the additional five acres were acquired. By 1975 seven cabins were completed. Thereafter, construction continued at a steady space with a total of 20 cabins eventually built.

The Summit provides a quiet haven for guests.
YMCA of the Rockies

Trouble in Paradise

The YMCA of the Rockies was not left untouched by social unrest that punctuated the 1960s. In 1967 the Association faced the first real threat to its authority by the college staff. In July Ruesch reported to the Board concerning "the resistance of certain agitators on the college staff to the existing rules and regulations...." The rules in question included "prohibition of drinking, of frequenting certain off-limits establishments where liquor is served and checking in and out of camp." To the horror of conservatives, "the college youth (were) requesting additional freedom in allowing members of the opposite sex in dormitory rooms."

Ruesch reported that resistance to the rules was nothing new, but this was the first time "it actually reached the point of open defiance...." The situation reached a climax when a "certain faction of the group demanded that the staff be allowed to present its ideas concerning these rules to the Board." This was completely unheard of, but because of the gravity of the situation Mr. Ruesch agreed to allow them to appear before members of the Employees Program and Welfare Committee. Mr. Ruesch agreed to this in a confrontation with the "agitators" during which he "reiterated his intention to continue to enforce the rules, even though such action might result in the necessity of sending a large group of them home and closing the camp."

After listening to the concerns, the Board issued its response. In part it stated, "...we have a responsibility to our guests... to promote a camp, Christian in character, where families and guests can enjoy their vacations in an atmosphere consistent with this image." Ruesch dealt with the problem with characteristic conviction. He told the Board "if I am to continue to operate the camp, I will do so only if these staff policies are continued, and only if I have the support of the Board of Directors in enforcing them." The Board quickly made a motion to support Ruesch which was unanimously passed.

Fewer than a handful of employees left rather than conform to the rules.

While Ruesch outwardly resisted the demands of the seasonal staff, there were some changes made in the YMCA's policies. During the late 1960s, management hired staff counselors who related to college students giving them channels for grievances. Staffers were more carefully screened and rules stated on a prearrival contract rather than disclosed upon arrival. During the early 1970s management softened its position concerning off grounds conduct of seasonal staff. However, management maintained standards of conduct by transferring responsibility to the staffer stating, "if your conduct on or off the grounds adversely affects your job, fellow staff members, guests, or the camp.... You are subject to dismissal."

Battle for the Administration Building

The rites of passage of youth in the sixties ran afoul of management in more humorous ways as well. The old stable had been remodeled into the Teen Barn. Ostensibly, it gave the teens a place to hang out, listen to music, and have dances. For the most part, the plan worked out well; however, there was one slight hitch. The Teen Barn is in an out of the way location. For the gregarious teens it was like being confined to jail. They wanted to be "where the action was" and that was the Administration Building. For the teenage girls it was especially important to be near the field where the boys of the Fellowship of Christian Athletes held their games.

Teens used the Ad Building as a place to sit, talk, play cards, and just watch the world go by. At an age when "hanging out" and "being seen" were so important, they sometimes occupied space needed for cabin guests and conference groups checking in or out. The teens were not subject to the same rules concerning dress, hair length, and behavior that governed the Association's staff. Their appearance and boisterous behavior sometimes offended the conservative administration as well as older guests.

Management did its best to discourage teens from using the Administration Building telling them to go to the Teen Barn. With an idealistic sense of fairness that only youth possess, they complained loudly. Some of their families had hung out at the Administration Building as youth and joined their children's protest. A truce was arrived at where the girls got to watch the boys, the boys got to watch the girls, and the teens got to continue hanging out at the "Ad." The only conditions were that they couldn't clog the steps with their presence and had to hold their youthful exuberance in check.

Keeping Step With the Times

To effectively deal with challenges of a changing society in the 1970s, the Board undertook long range planning including formulation of corporate goals. The task was primarily the responsibility of the Long Range Planning Committee; however, other Board Committees, outside consultants, and many staff members were actively involved. The result was a list of ten preliminary goals issued in November 1972. In part, they called for the allocation of resources to strengthen the family unit, to provide facilities for a wide range of conferences, and to become more closely allied with the larger YMCA Movement. Additional goals stressed balanced year-round operation, systematic financial development, effective public relations, and involvement in the communities of Estes Park and Granby.

Since goal formation is a constant process, the Board modified original goals and added others. Goals added in 1974 stressed the importance of Christian values, enrichment of conference offerings, and responsibilities to the college staff. Facilitation of goals was mainly visible in new program offerings and construction of new facilities at both Snow Mountain Ranch and Estes Park.

One of the new programs aimed at the changing social climate in America was the Estes Park Forum. The Forum was envisioned as an ongoing seminar to "make persons aware of the challenges facing our society, ecology, racism, religion, etc, and empower them to go back to their (home towns) and effect change." From the beginning the program was plagued with deficits and was discontinued after a short time.

Another offering was an outgrowth of the ecology movement and new consciousness of the times. The words "outdoor education" were first mentioned in official records of the Association in July 1972 when Program Director Norman Holstein suggested accommodating groups of area school children during the fall for that purpose. Walter Ruesch agreed seeing it as a way to increase business during the fall and spring seasons.

In 1973, 2,100 school children used facilities at Estes Park for outdoor education. Growing emphasis in that area continued when Dave Price who had a master's degree in outdoor education was hired as Program Director in 1975. The Association had obviously struck a positive chord as over 13,000 school children were served during 1975 and 1976.

The spider web, one of outdoor education's team building activities.
YMCA of the Rockies   Carl Scofield

During the next decade the experiment in outdoor education would prove to be a major success with 90 schools from Colorado and Wyoming utilizing the grounds. Programs were developed tailored to each group and their needs. The programs emphasized team-building and experiential "hands-on" learning through various activities including ropes course, orienteering, natural sciences, Native American study, fire ecology, animal adaptations, night awareness, beaver succession and pond exploration, and wilderness safety.

A growing awareness of the environment was also evident in other areas. The YMCA joined with the National Park Service in teaching environmental awareness at Sprague Lake through nature trails and educational games. By expanding the number of nature hikes around the grounds, an increasing number of guests were served who wanted to observe nature without taking long hikes. Conference groups such as the National Wildlife Federation started using the grounds and surrounding National Park as a giant outdoor classroom.

Seeking a Year-Round Operation

As the development of Snow Mountain Ranch placed increased demands on the Association, it became more important than ever to have a balanced twelve month cash flow. With summers at or near capacity at Estes Park, the only room for growth was in the remaining nine months. In 1969, Friendship was winterized for off season group use. Two years later several of the old circle cabins dating from the teens were winterized.

The payoff for the continued winterization program began to show in 1972 when 600 groups were accommodated outside the summer season. Increased use of the grounds during winter prompted winterization of both the Women's Building and Texas Building for meeting space. Christmas 1973 was an especially good time for the Estes Park Center with the grounds filled to capacity by groups and cabin guests. In 1977 the Administration Building was heated and insulated, replacing Sweet Memorial as the winter office.

Much of the YMCA's winter and especially holiday business depended on the availability of skiing. With Hidden Valley Ski Area on the wrong side of the Continental Divide for dependable snow, ski business was a hit and miss proposition at best. The winter of 1976 found visitors to many of the state's ski areas including Hidden Valley staring at rocks and bare ground. The next winter arrangements were made to transport skiers to Lake Eldora Ski Area where snow was more dependable. The winter of 1978 was a good snow year as reflected in increased winter business.

Fickle snows combined with increased sophistication of skiers who demanded more than was available at Hidden Valley, forced the YMCA to reposition itself in the winter market. As the 1970s came to a close, marketing was directed towards non-ski groups thus lessening the dependency on snow for winter business.

One of the needs previously identified at the Estes Park Center was lodges suitable for year round use by both youth and adult conference groups. Mt. Ypsilon Lodge was completed in July 1969. The three Eastside Lodges, Deer Ridge, Rainbow and Twin Sisters were completed on July 3, 1977 just as their first guests checked in.

No More Baths

In 1970 the bathhouse behind the Administration Building were closed. For decades they had served cabin and lodge guests whose accommodations lacked bathing facilities. Ostensibly, the bathhouse was anachronistic since all guests had access to adequate facilities. However, such was not totally the case. Ruesch revealed an underlying reason when he responded to queries stating, "the bathhouse was closed because of the increasing number of undesirable transients in the area, and the impossibility of supplying adequate supervision." Many of the seasonal staff lamented the passing of the bathhouse as it was the only place they could soak after a long hike since their dorms had only showers.

Water, Water Every Where and Not...

The 1970s were marked by several years of sparse snowfall. The most critical year was 1976-77. Lack of snow cover caused the spring that supplied a majority of the Estes Park Center's winter water to freeze leaving the grounds without water for several days. The drought persisted into summer forcing a cessation of all irrigation of lawns and necessitating other water conservation measures.

Guests had difficulty understanding the shortage since they saw the grounds two-thirds surrounded by running water. The problem was that none of that water belonged to the Estes Park Center. The YMCA was able to purchase rights to some of the Western Slope water flowing through the Adams Tunnel. Those water rights combined with a new water line assured enough water for present needs as well as those for the foreseeable future.

A Day to Remember

The summer of 1976 was eagerly anticipated in Colorado. The United States was celebrating its Bicentennial on July 4 while Colorado was to mark its Centennial on July 31. Centennial Day was a typical summer day in Estes Park. The morning dawned clear giving way to building thunderheads.

During early evening driving sheets of rain and intense lightning pummeled Estes Park. Most people familiar with summer storms in the mountains sought temporary shelter until the storm passed. Some found a place in front of the television set to watch the Summer Olympics where Sugar Ray Leonard had a scheduled boxing match.

People huddled in their motel rooms or tents were unaware of the drama being played out in the Big Thompson Canyon between Estes Park and Loveland. Ten to fourteen inches of rain fell on the upper Big Thompson Canyon and the North St. Vrain near Glen Haven. The normally placid Big Thompson and North St. Vrain Rivers became raging torrents as five million tons of water made its way towards the plains. While Estes Park slept, over 125 people lost their lives, and the property damage ran into the tens of millions of dollars. All celebrations of the Centennial were canceled.

Quickly the rumors started, fueled both by the press and hysteria. Many people thought all of Estes Park was wiped out including the Estes Park Center. The situation was worsened by a lack of telephone communications with the outside world.

The flood wiped out an entire week of revenue for the Estes Park Center including one major conference. As soon as telephone service was restored, staff contacted families who had booked accommodations later in the month telling them that Estes Park was unaffected. The Association's income was affected only slightly, but the psychological scars would last forever.

The Big Thompson Canyon, August 1, 1976.
Estes Park Trail Gazette   Tim Asbury

Preserving a Rich Heritage

When the intersection of Kallenberg and Rainbow drives was selected as the site for a new auditorium and conference dining room, old Wind River Lodge suffered the fate of many historically significant buildings. The land it occupied was just too valuable to justify its present use. The Lodge also suffered from age, neglect, and year round use for which it was never intended.

There was never a question as to the Lodge's historical significance. In 1973 the Wind River Memorial Committee reported that the Lodge was worthy of preservation. In July 1975 moving it to a new location for use as a museum was considered, but that was ruled out. Therefore, it was scheduled for demolition.

When Lula W. Dorsey learned of the impending destruction, she contacted Ruesch. At the July 1976 Board meeting, Lula Dorsey's offer was brought before the Board by Ruesch saying:

> ...although the Board decision has been made to tear Wind River Lodge down, the matter has been reopened to consider Miss Lula Dorsey's offer to finance the moving of the original section of the Lodge to a suitable site and making it into a museum.

The immediate question was whether it was more feasible to move it or tear it down and build a facsimile from the salvaged materials. The Board gave Ruesch the power to act accordingly to preserve what he could for a museum.

Ruesch determined that the original 1902 section was too structurally deteriorated to move. In November 1977 Ruesch reported that "Wind River is almost gone." The west end, built in 1924, was moved to the field back of the pool to house a museum, and the center section of the same vintage was moved to Mesa Drive for staff housing. On July 23, 1978 Alice Ruesch hosted a pre-dedication open house drumming up support for the project.

In June of 1979 the first curators of the Lula W. Dorsey Museum arrived to begin the task of opening the museum. Lulabeth and her husband Jack Melton were given the opportunity because of their knowledge of historic preservation and antiques. They also had been instrumental in convincing Lula Dorsey of the importance of saving the building.

Walter Ruesch took them to the unfinished and unfurnished museum. He also took them to various places where items were stored. Last, Ruesch handed them a set of pass keys, assurances of cooperation in whatever they needed, and introduced them to four young ladies who would work with them.

The next six weeks were spent in rummaging through storage areas, attics, basements, cabins, and file cabinets. Many pieces of furniture were refinished and repaired. The museum staff met the deadline, but in true YMCA style, some of the paint was not yet dry when the building was dedicated on July 29th!

The bulldozed remains of the original Wind River Lodge, October 1977.
Lula W. Dorsey Museum

The renovated 1924 addition made possible by Lula W. Dorsey.
YMCA of the Rockies   Carl Scofield

Walter G. Ruesch Auditorium

Since 1909 an adequate auditorium had been on the wish
lists of Board and management alike. Each time an auditorium
was constructed, it was built for the present rather than with
the future in mind. For a number of years Ruesch pushed for an
auditorium that would attract upscale groups. The Longhouse
was fine for youth groups but woefully inadequate for many
purposes. During corporate planning of the early 1970s, the
need for a true auditorium received endorsement. In 1972 the
Board appointed a special committee to study the location and
general plan for a 300 seat auditorium.

It was not until 1976 that the final concept began to take
shape. During the same period planning for a new conference
dining room was under way as well. At first, combining the two
was rejected on the grounds that the congestion would be
unmanageable. The two were eventually combined and the
auditorium plan enlarged to 800 seats. In March 1978, fund

raising was well underway. Farmland Industries pledged $60,000 to the project representing the single largest contribution.

Actual construction for the auditorium began in September 1977. Weather, problems with subcontractors, and last minute changes worked in unison to drive up the cost as well as to delay completion. After the Auditorium was dedicated on July 27, 1980, it proved an instant success with returning and prospective customers alike.

Ruesch Says Good Bye

The summer of 1980 marked the retirement of Walter G. Ruesch after 30 years of service to the YMCA of the Rockies. On the eve of his retirement, Ruesch reminisced. Among other things, he recalled that his first budget in 1950 was $150,000 while his last was $6,000,000. In remembering his tenure, he said, "We had no problems, just opportunities!" The coming years quickly offered many new "opportunities."

The Walter G. Ruesch Auditorium.
YMCA of the Rockies   Carl Scofield

The YMCA of the Rockies Goes Camping

A resident youth camp was envisioned since the purchase of the Just Ranch in 1966. With the opening of Camp Chief Ouray at Snow Mountain Ranch in 1980, a dream of many Board members and staff was fulfilled. The relocation of Camp Chief Ouray to Snow Mountain Ranch gave renewed life to an existing institution while adding new dimensions to another.

Roots of YMCA Camping

When Camp Chief Ouray opened in 1907, YMCA camping was already well developed in its objectives and programs. According to Eugene A. Turner Jr. who documented the history of YMCA camping in 100 Years of YMCA Camping, there is some question when YMCA camping actually began. However, as far back as 1867 boys camped out at Lake Champlain under the auspices of the Vermont YMCA. By the early to mid 1880s a number of YMCAs were taking boys camping.

The first camps were relatively small, serving just a handful of boys, and were usually less than two weeks in duration. Those early camps typically consisted of a number of tents set in a semicircle on the shores of a lake. Features included a never-dying campfire and flagpole. Bible study, physical activity, hearty meals, and fun in abundance quickly became earmarks of YMCA camping. Many camps had a military flavor with reveille, calisthenics before breakfast, and titles such as colonel for the camp director. Early YMCA camping was a rough affair with bathing in cold lakes and primitive living conditions.

Many camp directors and boards thought that was the way it should be; rough living built character.

Camp Chief Ouray

In 1907 three men, Stephen Knight, James H. Causey and Luman B. Hershey, purchased three acres of land two miles from Granby and 99 miles from Denver where Willow Creek runs into the Grand River (Colorado River). They presented the land to the Denver YMCA for a boys camp. Located on an old Ute Indian campground, it was named after a famous Ute chief, Ouray.

Chief Ouray was born near Taos, New Mexico in 1839 to a Jicarilla Apache mother and Ute father. He married Chipeta, known for her wisdom and gentleness. Ouray was a celebrated warrior who, by some accounts, once held 700 Arapahos at bay near Denver in 1858 with only 30 warriors. He fought numerous other battles with the Cheyenne and Sioux.

Chief Ouray lived near the Uncompaghre River south of Montrose, Colorado on a ranch given to him by the government in reward for helping stop the White River Massacre. There, living in a fine home, he adopted many trappings of white culture. While he was seen as a friend of the white, some Native Americans viewed him as a traitor. Ouray survived several attempts on his life by disgruntled tribesmen. In 1880 Ouray was called to Washington, D.C. to negotiate a peace treaty. As a present, Chipeta made an elaborately beaded and fringed buckskin shirt for her husband to wear.

The treaty was signed shortly before Ouray's death on August 24, 1880, ending the bloody Indian Wars of the 1860s and 1870s. The next year Arapahos, Cheyennes, and Utes moved to reservations. Thus, the man who gave the camp its name was more than a Native American whose personality lent a western air. He personified a Christian spirit whose love for his fellow man transcended cultural barriers.

The Camp's Early Years

Camp Chief Ouray hosted its first campers in 1908, under Mr. Jesse G. Arnold, the first camp director. The Camp's 1908 promotional brochure stated the purpose of the camp:

(The) object is to give a limited number of boys ages 12-17 a vacation in God's Out-of-Doors under competent, Christian leadership, and thereby gratify the natural desire of every normal boy for a free and easy out-of-door life....

Cost for the first year's camp was $10 per session or $16 for both sessions.

Campers slept in tents with pine boughs for mattresses. They cooked and ate in a tent nicknamed the "Big Top." They washed dishes and bathed in the cold water of an irrigation ditch. The "official" camp uniform was a blue flannel shirt, khaki pants, and tan leggings. Boys were instructed to bring:

...two heavy blankets, Bible, trousers, stockings, heavy shoes, one deep tin or granite plate, cup and saucer, one metal handle fork and knife, one spoon, toothbrush, comb, towels, soap, handkerchiefs, and towel for dishes.

The camper's outfit was packed in "a large denim bag with drawstring." The blankets were tightly rolled and roped. Trunks were not allowed.

A typical day in 1908 began with reveille at 6:30. A half hour of Bible study preceded breakfast at 7:30. Mornings were occupied with various sports. After lunch, hikes, fishing, nature study, and picture taking filled the afternoon hours. Another important feature was a man who knew Ouray and led campers in study of archaeology. Evenings found campers sitting around the campfire followed by an evening devotional.

The July 9, 1908 issue of the <u>Denver Young Men</u> said campers celebrated the 4th of July "with proper ceremonies and festivities, including ice cream..., to say nothing of the athletic stunts, consisting of track events, climbing the greased pole, and catching the greased pig." Every boy seemingly carried a "liberal allowance of fire works" for an evening display.

Patriotic observance was not limited to the 4th. The commandant of the Denver High School Cadets was in camp to teach attributes of a military camp including raising and saluting the flag as well as military style drills.

The first group of Camp Ouray campers was visited by William Jennings Bryan who was "stumping" during his third and final unsuccessful campaign for President. During his visit he thrilled the boys with colorful and interesting stories.

From modest beginnings the Camp quickly gained momentum. In 1909 boys were divided into groups of seven and assigned to an adult leader. Boys earned a Camp patch by showing competency in Bible study, nature study, and observance of camp rules. In 1909 horseback riding was added to the program. Parents were assured by camp literature as to the safety of the activity: "the horses we use will not be fiery, untamed mustangs of the plains, but animals which may be ridden with perfect assurance of safety." The horses quickly became an integral part of camp life. Many a camper's last stop when leaving was to say farewell to his favorite mount.

During the second year an addition was made that some campers surely did not view as an enhancement when the Camp got its first doctor. Rex B. Yeager, a student of the Denver University Medical School, endeared himself to campers by giving daily doses of castor oil!

Swimming in the cold waters of Schuyler Lake.
Courtesy Denver Metropolitan YMCA

Camp Chief Ouray hikers, circa 1920.
Courtesy Denver Metropolitan YMCA

Growth continued at a rapid pace during the teens. In 1915 the camping season was expanded to three sessions. Mothers reluctant about the quality of the food were assured that "the kitchen will be presided over by a motherly woman who will see that only the right kind of properly cooked foods are served." In 1917 an additional 37 acres was purchased. About the same time the program of CCO received a major boost with the addition of a lake. A gift of United States Senator Karl C. Schuyler, it was used for swimming and canoe lessons.

World War I saw Camp Chief Ouray doing its part for the war effort. The already regimented style of the Camp was given a very distinctive military flavor with military style drills and calisthenics. The Denver Young Men gave the rationale behind the military emphasis stating:

> If there ever was a time when the boys of our country needed to be led in their play and work so that they would become physically fit, mentally alert, socially safe, and spiritually guided, that time has come. With the best of our young manhood called to arms, leaving vacancies in the commercial world and in Christian leadership, our boys will be required to respond to demands for service that the boys of the past generation knew nothing about.

In 1918 the Lodge which was the trademark of old Camp Chief Ouray was built. It contained a dining room, kitchen, and store where boys bought candy, fishing tackle etc. The upstairs had several dorm rooms for parents or other visitors. There was also a "bank" where boys drew on money they brought to spend. That same year ten cabins were built in a group replacing the simple tents.

In 1920 the Denver YMCA gave CCO bragging rights calling it the "best camp west of the Mississippi." Literature further stated that over 1000 boys had been served, and the camping season was expanded to four sessions.

The old Lodge.
Courtesy Denver Metropolitan YMCA

Rustic cabins, circa 1918.
Courtesy Denver Metropolitan YMCA

A cabin group, circa 1918.
Courtesy Denver Metropolitan YMCA

Leaving Camp Chief Ouray for home.
Courtesy Denver Metropolitan YMCA

Checking the bull's-eye, circa 1935.
Courtesy Denver Metropolitan YMCA

Eating meals family style, 1942.
Courtesy Denver Metropolitan YMCA

The mid 1920s saw another round of improvements when an infirmary, library, dark room, and printing press for a Camp newspaper were added. In 1926 the Denver YMCA purchased the 360 acre McQueary Ranch adjoining the Camp. Renamed the Triangle-Y Ranch it supplied the Camp with milk, pork, and beef. As an added bonus a mile of Colorado River frontage gave campers access to some of the finest trout fishing waters in the state. In 1928 a crafts building and several duplex cabins were added. A major addition of the decade was a shower house with hot running water!

The Camp continued to grow and prosper, surviving even the difficult times of the Great Depression. The post World War II baby boom kept CCO packed during the late 1940s and 1950s. However, during the following decades YMCA camping in general fell on tough times. During those years of social change, many resident youth camps ceased operations. CCO continued to enjoy the support of Denverites and the business community. With new legislation and increased governmental regulation on all levels, CCO faced capital demands that it had difficulty meeting.

In May 1972 John R. Johnson, General Director of the Denver YMCA, contacted the YMCA of the Rockies concerning a joint venture in resident youth camping. Since a resident youth camp was envisioned for the Just ranch, it seemed logical that the two Associations not compete; however, no definite action was taken.

The topic again came to the forefront in February 1978 when representatives of the Denver YMCA and YMCA of the Rockies met. During the meeting various uses of a new camp were discussed including dialysis camps, diabetic camps, and outdoor education. Talk also centered around ingredients for a successful camp operation, budgets, subsidies, as well as disposal of the old Camp Chief Ouray.

Ruesch informed the Executive Committee that immediate action was required so that operation of Camp Chief Ouray could commence at Snow Mountain Ranch by the summer of 1980.

The full Board approved the transfer at the July meeting. In April 1979 Ruesch presented an architect's renderings of the proposed buildings.

Chipeta dining hall and sleeping cabins were finished in time for use by the campers in June 1980. The Everitt Foundation provided funding for a health center. The official dedication was held on July 24, and during the first season 700 boys and girls were accommodated. A special dialysis camp utilizing equipment furnished by Denver General Hospital allowed five children who could not otherwise do so attend camp.

The YMCA of the Rockies now had its own resident youth camp with roots deep in traditional YMCA camping. However, very quickly Camp Chief Ouray would develop new programs and directions meeting the demands of a changing society while maintaining service to youth.

Flag raising at the new Camp Chief Ouray.
YMCA of the Rockies

Riding the Roller Coaster

The early 1980s were anything but an amusement ride for the YMCA of the Rockies. The Association found itself caught up in spiraling interest rates, rising utility costs, inflation, and growing economic recession affecting the entire nation. By mid March of 1980 the economy was in a state of shock as the prime interest rate hit 20% and treasury bills were at 16%. Despite the economy, many new facilities were added at Snow Mountain Ranch, Camp Chief Ouray, and Estes Park Center.

Things Get Critical

The effect of the downturn in the world economy on the YMCA was dramatic. The "mini-gasoline scare" of 1979 forced many guests to cancel their reservations. At the Estes Park Center, the effect of the gas crunch was negligible as empty beds were quickly filled with Coloradoans looking for vacations close to home. Snow Mountain Ranch with its perceived isolation on the Western Slope was harder hit. The problem was compounded by double digit inflation in 1980 which caused numerous group cancellations.

The obvious method of coping with the situation was to cut all unnecessary expenditures. Unfortunately, during the previous two years, the Board had accelerated a program of capital projects. New construction projects totaling $3,000,000 were due for completion by June, 1980. When several of the projects went over budget because of last minute changes and problems with sub-contractors, that figure increased.

The debt load of the Association was increased further in 1980 when the YMCA purchased the 2000 acre Broderick property adjacent to Snow Mountain Ranch. The parcel first came up for sale in 1972 but no action was taken. During the ensuing years commercial logging took place on the land. Disturbing and dangerous logging traffic annoyed guests and staff alike. Acquiring the land was also viewed as vital to the interests of the Association, to protect it from possible future commercial development. However, the ten year note with its $200,000 annual principal and interest payment weighed heavily on the Association.

Another blow to the Association's financial situation came on February 11, 1981, when Fairchild and Chiquita dorms in the Mummy Quadrangle were destroyed by fire. The Estes Park Volunteer Fire Department in conjunction with Estes Park Center employees fought the fire in twenty below zero temperatures. Their efforts were also hampered by fifty mile per hour winds.

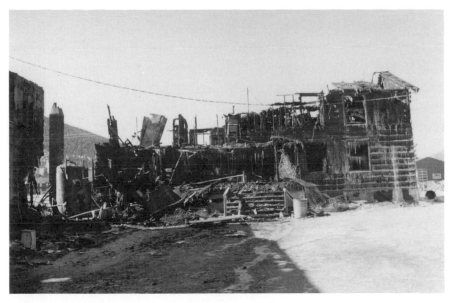

The icy remains of Fairchild Dormitory.
Lula W. Dorsey Museum   Lulabeth Melton

The loss of much needed employee housing was only part of the problem resulting from the fire. In a domino effect, displaced staff spilled into beds already rented for the next summer. If something was not done quickly, contracts with conference groups might have to be canceled. The Board's action was quick and decisive. Plans were drawn, bids taken, and ground broken on Eagle Cliff Lodge. Amazingly, it was finished in ninety days with guests checking in only hours after work was completed!

As if to add insult to injury, in late spring Melrose Cabin was gutted by fire shortly after it was cleaned and readied for opening. Faced with the same problem of previously rented bed space, Melrose was rebuilt in time for the summer season.

In August, 1981 Treasurer of the Board, Herbert Willborn, reported that "we are in an emergency, but not in a critical emergency...." Executive Director DeWitt Smith and his staff moved quickly in response to the financial situation. In actions reminiscent of the Depression, unneeded buildings were closed and nonessential staff furloughed. Willborn was complimentary of staff actions but expressed concern over uncontrollable expenses. He informed the Board that during the previous five years food costs had risen 17%, utilities 138%, room service supplies 77%, property taxes 44%, and insurance 41%. Willborn voiced the opinion of his fellow Board members and staff alike when in closing he stated, "we still remain optimistic about our future."

At the same Board meeting DeWitt Smith presented a paper concerning the possibility of refinancing the YMCA's debts under an Industrial Revenue Bond. With the cooperation of Grand County, a $2,000,000 bond issue was approved in 1982. It consolidated several loans, some of which carried 20% interest.

In spite of the bond issue, things did not immediately turn around for the Association. Continuing inflation and a deep recession kept the revenue side of the Association's ledger depressed. Willborn again alerted the Board to the problems in November, 1983 stating, "this is the first time I've had to give a report on the financial statement in the red." Although the situation was serious, Willborn was obviously not panicking saying, "the economy has taken a turn that we are going to have to adjust for until it turns around." Even the weather conspired against the YMCA during the previous winter when untimely, heavy snows caused numerous cancellations.

While Willborn reported on the red ink, Executive Director Smith optimistically described how staff had recently traveled to the East Coast, Midwest, and Southwest promoting the YMCA to prospective customers. He reported that there were positive responses boding well for the future. It was agreed that a major key to turning things around was to increase revenues through marketing. Smith further stated that the YMCA needed a full time marketing person. Marketing the YMCA was not an easy proposition. Over built Colorado ski resorts were in fierce competition with the YMCA for both winter and summer business.

There were no magic fixes in store for the YMCA. Operating deficits from required expenditures pushed the debt load upward. The economy remained depressed. Uncontrollable expenses such as taxes, insurance, and sewage disposal continued to escalate. The YMCA found breathing room in refinancing its debt, including the previous bonds, into a new Industrial Revenue Bond funded in 1985.

The Denver Office Closes

Since 1908 the YMCA of the Rockies had maintained the Corporate office at the downtown Denver YMCA. Every May the entire office including files, equipment, and personnel moved to Estes Park for the summer. In September the operation was reversed. The twice yearly moves were time consuming and expensive.

The Denver office was moved to a suburban location after the retirement of Walter Ruesch in 1980. When Executive Director DeWitt Smith moved to the Midwest Field Office, the

Denver office was closed entirely as a cost cutting measure. In the spring of 1985, files and equipment were loaded up one last time and hauled to Estes Park. The Camp Chief Ouray office was moved to Snow Mountain Ranch.

The move caused an office space crunch at Estes Park where room had to be found for seven positions. The basement of the Administration Building was remodeled to accommodate the Group Sales Office and Marketing. Two, two bedroom cabins were taken off the rental charts and turned into offices housing the Executive Director, Executive Secretary, Accountant, and Payroll clerk.

The YMCA Reaches Out

One of the highlights of the 1980s was the growing involvement of the YMCA of the Rockies outside of its direct sphere of influence. In 1980 the Association was designated an International YMCA. Not content with that achievement, the Board moved to complete requirements to have the Association named an International Program Center.

The focal point of the YMCA of the Rockies' growing involvement in the International Movement came in July, 1981 when the Estes Park Center hosted the 8th meeting of the World Alliance of YMCAs. Meeting under the theme "Christ: Renewal and Hope," 78 countries answered the opening roll call in the Ruesch Auditorium. For nine days, the Estes Park Center reflected the world's cultural diversities. Language barriers dissolved as delegates experienced international brotherhood and Christian fellowship.

The World Alliance meeting almost overshadowed an important conference preceding it. For five days 158 youth representing five continents gathered at the World Youth Conference. The conference was organized to stimulate involvement of youth in leadership positions in their respective YMCAs. It provided avenues of communication between youth and the World Council.

Language and cultural barriers dissolve in the spirit of brotherhood.
Lula W. Dorsey Museum

Other involvement in the International YMCA Movement saw the YMCA of the Rockies supporting efforts to establish a YMCA in Senegal. The YMCA of the Rockies also began assisting the Sioux Indian YMCA in Dupree, South Dakota.

In July 1984 it was announced that the Estes Park Center would host the Centennial of YMCA Camping. From September 30 through October 3, 650 persons attended the Centennial; the keynote speaker was Art Linkletter. The conference closed by burying a time capsule at the Lula W. Dorsey Museum to be opened in 2085 at the Bicentennial of YMCA Camping.

The crowning jewel of the growing internationalism of the YMCA of the Rockies occurred in 1987 when the Estes Park Center hosted the World Wilderness Congress. Even though it was not a YMCA affiliated conference, it united in brotherhood representatives from 26 countries including five heads of state seeking to protect the world's wildlife. For a week the eyes of the world were focused on the Estes Park Center via satellite.

The YMCA Celebrates its 75th Anniversary

In the midst of the economic problems of the early 1980s, the YMCA of the Rockies stopped to reflect on its heritage. In 1981, a 75th Anniversary Committee comprised of staff from both centers began planning the celebration scheduled for July 1982. The Lula W. Dorsey Museum staff worked to complete <u>YMCA of the Rockies: Seventy-Five Years of History 1907 - 1982</u>. As in 1957, staff and guests participated in a commemorative hike from Grand Lake to Estes Park. There was an anniversary banquet and other special events.

In conjunction with the 75th Anniversary the Board resolved to raise $1,250,000. The campaign was the largest and most successful in the Association history widely supported by Board, staff, members, alumni, and friends of the Association.

One Step Forward and One Back

One of the solutions to the decline in popularity of YMCA camping in the 1970s was the advent of specialty camping which catered to specific groups. In 1981 Camp Chief Ouray moved into the specialty camping field when it hosted its first Women's Fitness Camp. Scheduled in early June before the traditional camping season, the new camp was filled to capacity.

The dormitory style housing built at Camp Chief Ouray in 1980 proved unsuitable. It broke with the tradition of YMCA camping whereby small groups of children lived together in a cabin setting. Bonding and a sense of togetherness were difficult to establish in the dormitory setting. Some proponents of traditional camp housing said the new Camp Chief Ouray accommodations were "too plush." They felt that some type of platform tent housing was needed "to give the children a more typical camp living experience." Association friends, Mr. Edward Gaylord and Helen Bisgard, contributed funds necessary to build a traditional style village which opened in June, 1985.

Snow Mountain Ranch Continues to Grow

While there was a fifty year debate over the need for a swimming pool at the Estes Park Center, there was never any question that one would be built at Snow Mountain Ranch. In 1978 Board Member William L. Carter Jr. and his committee were finalizing construction details and fund raising plans for the pool. When Carter died unexpectedly in October, 1978, Walter Ruesch suggested naming the pool in his memory.

The William L. Carter Jr. Memorial Swimming Pool was opened for the summer of 1981. The Carter Pool not only provided a new activity for guests, it allowed Snow Mountain Ranch to reach out into the surrounding Middle Park communities. Lap swimming, swimming lessons, and swimnastics gave local residents something to help ward off the doldrums of the long mountain winters.

William L. Carter Jr. Memorial Swimming Pool.
YMCA of the Rockies

Rowley Homestead Museum and Nature Center.
YMCA of the Rockies

Governor's Cup race at Snow Mountain Ranch.
Winter Park   Rod Walker

In 1972 Martha and Ken Clark funded stabilization of the Rowley homestead cabin for future use as a museum. In 1983 SMR staff reported that a smokehouse, root cellar, and Mormon haystacker had been rebuilt. Daily tours were being conducted for guests. Later, a trapper's cabin was moved to the site and rebuilt with a sod roof. Several pieces of farm machinery were put on display and a windmill put in working order.

Incredible growth in Nordic skiing continued through the 1980s, and an expanding interest in fitness and increasing downhill lift ticket costs combined to place SMR at the pinnacle of a developing market. In 1984 the Nordic program which had outgrown its facilities was relocated to Camp Chief Ouray where Chipeta Dining Hall gave them plenty of elbow room. The Colorado Governors Cup race was held at SMR during the winter of 1984-85.

In 1985 Snow Mountain Ranch was named as the training center for the U.S. Biathlon team. Skiing programs for the physically challenged, youth, and adults covered all segments of the population. In response to the growing use of the trails, snow grooming equipment was purchased.

The Nordic Center continued to gain in popularity. It was the training center for both the U.S. Biathlon and U.S. Ski Teams in 1986. Adult mentally challenged, Special Olympic, and senior citizen groups were added to the growing list of users. Program and Camp Chief Ouray Director Kent Meyer reported that 8,400 people had used the trails during the winter of 1985-86, which doubled the previous year's total.

Since the opening of Snow Mountain Ranch, a miniature golf course had been on the Association's wish list. During the ensuing years, the project was not forgotten, just shuffled around. Initially, plans called for it to be an indoor course located in the basement of the Program Building. When that space was occupied by Flanagan's Ski Rental, the golf course was left without a home. Finally, in 1986, Snow Mountain Ranch dedicated the outdoor miniature golf course, Wendel's Ley Out.

Wendel's Ley Out.
YMCA of the Rockies

Carl Scofield

The Roller Coaster Ride Ends

The break that Board and staff were waiting for came in 1985 when it was reported that a budgeted excess revenue of $829,000 had grown to $1,100,000! However, the recent economic challenges served as a reminder to the Association of how fragile success was. Through sound fiscal management with capital expenditures put on a "pay as you go basis" the Association's financial affairs were put in order within two years.

As the YMCA of the Rockies emerged from the shadow of economic problems, the Board promoted Gene Garris to Executive Director in 1987. He provided an insight into the organization dating back to his days as a seasonal employee beginning in 1962. Together, Board, management, and staff began the process of prioritizing the needs of the Association to carry it into the next century.

The Future Starts Today

The YMCA of the Rockies wasted no time as it emerged from the doldrums created by the economic recession of the early and mid 1980s. The Association began systematically raising funds for a multitude of projects. During the three years between 1988 and 1991, $4,275,000 was spent on capital projects. By 1992, the Association had another $6,000,000 in projects under construction or on the drawing boards to continue fulfilling its mission of serving families, conferences, youth, and staff.

Priorities '88

During the winter of 1987, the various departments at Snow Mountain Ranch, Estes Park Center, and Camp Chief Ouray began compiling a capital projects wish list. Three were identified as the most pressing. The Estes Park Center desperately needed additional family reunion accommodations. The more than 300 family reunions hosted annually kept existing facilities booked two years in advance during the summer season. Snow Mountain Ranch needed a water storage reservoir since lack of a dependable water supply was one of the single biggest hindrances to expansion. There was a need for new cabins at Estes Park, and existing cabins at both centers were in need of renovation. The projects were approved by the Board of Directors and bundled together in the Priorities '88 campaign.

Pattie Hyde Barclay Reunion Lodge

The descendants of A.A. Hyde stepped forth with an offer to fund the major portion of the family reunion lodge in memory of Pattie Hyde Barclay, youngest daughter of A.A. Hyde. They were joined by many other friends of the Association, Board Members, staff, and guests.

Pattie Hyde Barclay first visited the YMCA in 1913 with her father. Like him and many others since, she fell in love with the mountains. In 1919 she married William Houston Barclay, and together the family enjoyed camping, hiking, birding, and woodcarving. It was within this framework of traditional family values that the lodge was dedicated.

As soon as plans for the Barclay Lodge were finalized, the Group Sales Office began renting space to eager families. Consequently, before the YMCA broke ground in the fall of 1989, the lodge was completely sold out for the summer of 1990.

Renewing family ties at the Pattie Hyde Barclay Reunion Lodge.
YMCA of the Rockies   Carl Scofield

From its spacious decks the Pattie Hyde Barclay Reunion Lodge offers sweeping views of the surrounding peaks. There are 16 bedrooms with baths including two handicapped accessible plus a bunk room with two baths accommodating a total of 70 individuals. The large dining room is separated from the lounge area by a massive native stone fireplace open on two sides. There is a fully equipped kitchen. Other facilities include an outdoor grill, picnic tables, coin-operated laundry, and playground. Only one group at a time uses Barclay Lodge assuring a quality experience.

The Gaylord Reservoir

During the 1980s, "water rights" became a buzz word throughout Colorado. Developing communities along the Front Range were battling agricultural interests for an increasingly scarce commodity. A 1981 Property Development Committee report stated "our water supply has absolute top priority." With that statement the Board of Directors began the lengthy and expensive process of acquiring, developing, and protecting water rights necessary to build a reservoir. Association friend Edward Gaylord provided the majority of the funding for the reservoir. Construction began in the spring of 1991 and was finished in time to catch the runoff of melting snows from the winter of 1991-92.

Cabin Renovations

Maintaining over 200 cabins at the Estes Park Center and 42 at Snow Mountain Ranch is a never ending proposition. By the late 1980s some cabin donors' priorities had expired both at Snow Mountain Ranch and Estes Park. These "orphaned" cabins were in need of rehabilitation. At Estes Park there were numerous old two bedroom cabins in need of immediate remodeling or removal.

The newly renovated Valley View cabin.
YMCA of the Rockies   Carl Scofield

With such wide ranging needs the cabin renovation portion of the Priorities '88 campaign took on several forms. Two bedroom cabins built in the 1950s and 1960s were "adopted" by new donors who added a bedroom and bath as well as new appliances, furniture, and carpet. Several donors whose priorities were about to expire remodeled their cabins. At Snow Mountain Ranch priorities had expired on several cabins. They were adopted and remodeled as well.

One of the biggest successes of the campaign was the adoption of many small two bedroom cabins at Estes Park. Some of them dated back to 1910 and had not received significant attention since the 1950s. They were adopted by new donors and given extensive renovation that will see their useful life extended to their 100th birthday.

As in previous decades, some friends of the Association were not satisfied with remodeling existing cabins. Phyllis and Harold Roffmann and Julie and Rick Johnson chose to build two bedroom cabins to serve as prototypes for small cabins in the future. Other donors built several new three and four bedroom cabins at the Estes Park Center.

The cabin building and adoption portion of the Priorities '88 campaign was so successful that the program was extended past the conclusion of the parent campaign.

All Under One Roof

While the constituency of the YMCA of the Rockies was busy surpassing the goals of the Priorities '88 campaign, the Board took on another challenge. Ever since relocation of the Corporate Office to Estes Park in 1985, there had been a shortage of adequate office space. Personnel added after the move compounded the situation. The Board recognized that the problem needed to be resolved immediately.

Board Member Lee Schlessman provided the major funding for a new office building through the Schlessman Family Foundation. Schlessman was followed by the entire Board of Directors who underwrote the remainder of the construction cost. With completion of the Schlessman Executive Offices in November of 1989 all Corporate functions of the Association were under one roof. For the first time in many years there was adequate office, storage, and meeting space.

Marketing the YMCA

For many years, the Association concerned itself with marketing only during times of economic stress. The rest of the time telephones rang constantly with groups and families wanting to use the two centers. During the 1970s and 1980s several factors came together forcing the YMCA to look at marketing itself in a professional and logical manner. Colorado's overbuilt ski areas became increasingly active in promoting themselves during the non-ski seasons. Many large hotel chains, cities, and even small resorts began marketing themselves as conference centers.

In 1984 a strategy verification and evaluation was conducted by W.E. McCabe and Associates. They issued a report that was presented to the Executive Director in November, 1984. Most of their suggestions were implemented along with others suggested by staff. During the mid and late 1980s the Association conducted numerous in-house surveys to determine exactly who uses the grounds and why.

Out of these two elements, a marketing plan was developed for the YMCA with the objective of generating additional family and conference reservations, promoting use of facilities during non-peak periods, and increasing use of Camp Chief Ouray. The plan was carried out through research, staff training, publications, direct mail, public relations, and in-house communications. An additional area focused on representation of the YMCA at consumer and trade shows.

The Information Age

During the early 1970s a special committee was appointed to study computerization of the Association's business operations. The cost and complexity of computer systems of the day prevented immediate action. At the beginning of the 1980s the Association purchased its first reservations computer for the Estes Park Center. The system was put into operation in 1981. Immediately, problems in the software sent guest registrars back to the old tried and true paper charts. The problems were eventually worked out and the system took over many tasks such as tracking reservations, posting charges, and billing long distance telephone calls to rooms or cabins.

The Association's accounting procedures were still handled using traditional methods until 1983 when an accounting computer and software were acquired. The room sized computer generated enough heat and noise to make it almost unbearable to operate. In 1988 it was finally replaced with IBM personal computers linked together in a network.

Correspondence was still carried out using typewriters except for the Dorsey Museum which used an Apple computer. The Association kept buying increasingly sophisticated and expensive typewriters, but they were no substitute for word processors. In 1986 the YMCA purchased a used IBM word processor. The machine was slow, but it was better than a typewriter.

The growing importance of marketing highlighted the need for computerized mailing lists. For several years that task was contracted to a firm in Denver. The firm and its data entry personnel sometimes caused the Association many headaches when members failed to receive reservation mailings. Consequently, in 1987 the YMCA purchased a used IBM personal computer and laser printer bringing the task in house.

In 1987, management recognized that the Estes Park Center reservation computer was totally obsolete. Management also determined that Snow Mountain Ranch, which had no reservation computer, needed one. In 1988 a computer task force was formed and charged with the responsibility of determining the needs of the Association. The task force determined that the best system was one comprised of IBM compatible computers linked together in networks. Today, the entire operation of the YMCA of the Rockies has been automated. There are scores of computers linked together sharing information on an Association wide basis.

Vacation Kidney Center

In 1988 the YMCA of the Rockies forged ahead in a bold endeavor. Since 1975, kidney dialysis was available to Camp Chief Ouray attendees during a special one-week camp; however, it was on a very limited basis. The first year only two patients received dialysis. In 1976, University Hospital of Denver furnished a motor home equipped with portable dialysis machines. That summer six campers on dialysis went to camp.

When the YMCA of the Rockies reopened Camp Chief Ouray at Snow Mountain Ranch, the one-week dialysis camp continued utilizing the Everitt Health Center. Outside of the special camp for children, vacationing in Grand County for those on dialysis was totally out of the question.

In a cooperative effort the University Hospital of Denver, the National Kidney Foundation of Colorado, and the YMCA of the Rockies began shaping the unique concept of a vacation dialysis center at Snow Mountain Ranch. The National Kidney Foundation provided funds for the building, University Hospital provided the medical expertise and equipment necessary to operate the unit, and the YMCA provided the land, utilities, and labor to build the dialysis center.

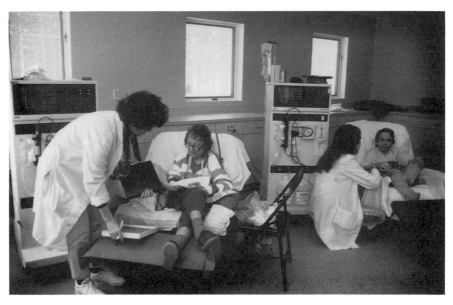

Two guests receive dialysis.
YMCA of the Rockies

The Marcia Murphy Lortscher National Kidney Foundation Vacation Kidney Center was dedicated on March 9, 1991. It was named in honor of Mrs. Marsha Lortscher, the longest living kidney transplant recipient, who was instrumental in helping obtain the cooperation of the National Kidney Foundation. Other participants in making the Vacation Kidney Center a reality were the Helen K. and Arthur E. Johnson Foundation, Dane Hansen Foundation, Peter H. and E. Lucille Gaass Kuyper Foundation, and patrons of the YMCA of the Rockies.

The Vacation Kidney Center provides facilities for expanded use of Camp Chief Ouray by campers on dialysis. It also makes dialysis a reality for guests of Snow Mountain Ranch, others vacationing in Grand County, and Grand County residents.

Taking the Bite Out of Taxes

Coping with rising property taxes has occupied many hours of the Board and management's time during the last decade. However, problems with property taxes were not limited to the modern era. As early as 1913 the YMCA fought to keep its property free of taxes. After lengthy legal negotiations Larimer County was prohibited from collecting taxes on the YMCA property "in perpetuity."

The property tax question remained status quo until 1941 when the YMCA agreed to pay taxes based on a 10% commercial usage of its facilities. The agreement was not based on Colorado law but rather an informal agreement. In 1970 several Estes Park accommodation owners complained to Larimer County that the low tax rate gave the Association an unfair advantage. In a 1971 ruling, the Colorado Tax Commission ruled that the YMCA of the Rockies was no longer exempt from full taxation.

During the following years the property was reevaluated and the Association was subject to spiraling taxes of the 1970s and 1980s. Property taxes at Estes Park crested at $400,000. In June 1990, the Association sought help from professionals in the field of property tax abatement. They determined that the Larimer County Assessor failed to comply with appraisal standards and guidelines established in the Colorado Property Tax Administrator's rules and regulations. The Assessor was also unwilling to acknowledge that the Estes Park Center was a lodging facility and should be valued in the same manner as other lodging properties in the county.

Lengthy negotiations including a hearing before the State Board of Assessment Appeals resulted in the taxes on the Estes Park Center being reduced by 40%. Management took steps to have the rollback applied to taxes for 1988, 1989, and 1990. After paying legal fees and a percentage to the company representing the YMCA, the Association netted $250,000. The savings were immediately earmarked for maintenance at the Estes Park Center. In 1992 the YMCA began taking necessary steps to obtain revaluation of property at Snow Mountain Ranch. Any savings will likewise be used for maintenance of facilities at Snow Mountain Ranch.

The Legacy of Camp Chief Ouray Continues

By the time the YMCA of the USA celebrated its centennial of camping in 1984, over 1,500,000 children and nearly 300,000 adults took advantage of the opportunities of YMCA resident and day camps on a yearly basis. Today, Camp Chief Ouray serves over 1,500 youth in its residence youth camp, leadership training programs, and hiking programs. The program at Camp Chief Ouray is designed to provide fun and growth for children. Special attention is given to the development of positive human relations, leadership, and Christian values. Camp Chief Ouray offers eight one-week sessions for boys and girls ages 8 through 16. Additionally, there is one special ten-day Teen Session offered for campers aged 13 to 16.

While many facets of the Camp have changed since 1907 some have not. Campers are housed in a cabin setting with a counselor, an assistant and seven or eight other children of their own age and sex. Campers awaken at 7 a.m. and spend the next hour and a half cleaning the cabin and performing work for the good of the group. Breakfast, like all meals, is served family style in Chipeta Dining Hall. Mornings are spent in various activities. After lunch there is quiet time followed by an activity period. Before supper there is an hour spent with the cabin group in special activities. Following the evening meal, campers participate in games. Every day is closed by the traditional evening campfire and vesper time.

Many of the activities participated in by youth today are the same as in the early days including archery, riflery, crafts, games, horseback riding, swimming, nature study, music, orienteering, and fishing. However, some activities such as mountain biking, rafting, and a ropes challenge course might seem strange to the camper of 1907.

Camp Chief Ouray places special emphasis on hiking and backpacking through its Trekker, Sherpas and Colorado Trail programs. Trekkers ages 12-14 set up a base camp in Arapaho National Forest where they spend three days exploring the surrounding wilderness. Sherpas ages 13-15 spend four days and three nights backpacking through the Colorado wilderness. The Colorado Trail program for ages 14-16 participate in a wilderness living experience spending six days and five nights hiking along the Colorado Trail.

Camp Chief Ouray offers four Leadership Training Programs designed for young people who wish to develop their leadership skills. Emphasis is placed on skills needed to be a camp counselor. The three-week programs develop leadership and camper relationship skills through education, observation, involvement, and actual experience with cabin groups and camp activities.

The Leader-In-Training (LIT) program is for those who have completed the 8th grade and have a desire to work with children in camp a setting. LIT emphasizes group interaction, personal worth, and confidence while working in both small and large groups.

Youth who have completed the 9th, 10th, or 11th grades may participate in the Specialist-In-Training (SIT) program. SIT is designed for those who wish to develop expertise in hiking, mountain biking, and horseback riding for future use in a camp setting.

The Counselor-In-Training (CIT) program is for those who have completed the 10th or 11th grades. CITs participate in a week of training before spending two weeks as a member of a cabin group. CITs assist the counselors in leadership of the cabin and camp activities.

The last leadership training program is the Sioux Indian YMCA Service Project. Participants who have completed the 9th, 10th, or 11th grades combine the fun of camp with the rewards of community service. After spending time at Camp Chief Ouray to prepare activities and develop personal and group goals, these youth travel to the Sioux Indian Reservation in Dupree, South Dakota. There they work to provide young Native Americans with an on-site day camp experience.

Camp Chief Ouray is at the crux of YMCA camping, branching out into specialty camping with Active Older Adult and Women's Fitness Camps. The Active Older Adult Camp is held after the last youth session in August. Seventy-five adults "at least 50 years young" participate in a wide variety of daily activities. After rising campers swim, walk, or animal watch followed by a morning devotion and flag raising. Breakfast like all meals for campers at CCO is served family style. Before lunch activities include aerobics, hiking, archery, or mountain biking. Afternoons are spent in free time, horseback riding, tennis, hiking, card games, or Aquacise. Evening activities include strolls, vespers, hayrides, sing-a-longs, and games.

The second specialty camp at Camp Chief Ouray is Women's Fitness Camp. Two camps for 100 each have the goal of helping women make a commitment to a personal fitness program. Days are full of activities including lap swimming, walking or jogging, T'ai Chi, yoga, swimnastics, riding, hiking, archery, aerobics, lunch, volleyball, crafts, and lectures. The week is uncluttered by family, cooking, and other everyday chores.

Camp Chief Ouray has a long tradition of serving the needs of boys and girls to grow in body, mind, and spirit while having fun in the out-of-doors. As the demographics of our society change, Camp Chief Ouray will continue to develop new specialty camps to address changing needs.

A cabin group plays ball.
YMCA of the Rockies   Carl Scofield

Newly made friends ham it up at Camp Chief Ouray.
YMCA of the Rockies   Carl Scofield

Camper and her counselor enjoy mountain biking.
YMCA of the Rockies   Carl Scofield

Learning a new skill builds confidence for camper.
YMCA of the Rockies   Carl Scofield

From Experiment to Major Success

The wisdom of experimenting with Nordic skiing at Snow Mountain Ranch has continued in the 1990s. The Nordic Center is open six months, but Blue Ridge on Snow Mountain Ranch offers nine months of nordic skiing from October to early June.

The Snow Mountain Ranch Nordic Center offers cross country skiing for skiers of all ages and abilities on 85 kilometers of cross country ski trails that wind through mountain valleys and stands of lodgepole pine, aspen, and sub-Alpine fir. There is even a lighted 2.6 kilometer loop for night skiing.

Snow Mountain Ranch normally hosts several competitive Nordic events each year. Competitors range in age from 5 years to 70 plus, and races vary in length from 5 kilometers to a 42 kilometer marathon. Local racers, public school teams, and collegiate teams use the Nordic Center for training purposes. The Nordic Center boasts one of only three permanent biathlon ranges in the western United States.

The Changing Face of Seasonal Staff

The seasonal staff at the Estes Park Center numbers 325 during the summer and 65 during the other nine months. Snow Mountain Ranch employs 135 seasonals during the summer and 100 from September to May. Long gone are the days when the seasonal staff of the YMCA of the Rockies was mostly white, female, college age, and from the Midwest.

The summer staff of the Estes Park Center in 1991 reflected the diversification of today's seasonal staff. The junior staff consisted of 110 women and 80 men. The aging of the American population combined with many individuals taking early retirement is the basis for one of the biggest changes in the makeup of the staff. In 1991, there were 17 married couples, 48 adult women, and 10 adult men on the staff.

Whereas the seasonal staff was once recruited primarily from the ranks of Student YMCAs, today's staff comes to the

YMCA of the Rockies from a variety of sources. Word of mouth from family or friends brings fully one-third of the staff to work at the YMCA. Other sources include recruiting guests from earlier years, college placement offices, YMCAs, and magazine or newspaper articles.

It is not unusual for both centers to employ individuals from over 20 countries including England, France, Germany, Japan, Togo, Thailand, Columbia, Brazil, Czechoslovakia, Commonwealth of Independent States, Scotland, Denmark, Hungary, Switzerland, Nepal, Ivory Coast, Morocco, Mexico, Italy, Australia, New Zealand, and Canada. While language and cultural differences sometimes initially present problems, those barriers are quickly broken down through the spirit of kinship and love.

A Snapshot of Today

The Estes Park Center encompasses 860 acres in a setting long acclaimed as the most scenic in the Rocky Mountains. There are over 200 cabins and 16 group lodging accommodations available. A maximum of 3,400 people can be accommodated at one time during the summer. Dining facilities can serve over 11,000 meals per day. In 1991, 15,000 reservations representing over 50,000 individuals were made through the guest reservation office. Over 1,000 groups consisting of 57,000 people utilized the grounds.

Snow Mountain Ranch is situated on 4,400 acres. It offers a combination of historic setting and modern facilities. Once envisioned as a vast winter playground, Snow Mountain Ranch is today busy year around. There are 42 cabins, 39 campsites, and 9 group lodges. A maximum of 1,500 can be housed at one time. In 1991, 11,000 reservations representing 35,000 individuals were made through the guest reservation office. Over 600 groups consisting of almost 23,000 people stayed at Snow Mountain Ranch.

Both Snow Mountain Ranch and the Estes Park Center offer a wide range of program activities to suit the varying tastes of guests. At the Estes Park Center, Rocky Mountain National Park, thousands of acres of National Forest land, and the diversions in nearby Estes Park round out the leisure time offerings. Snow Mountain Ranch offers similar program activities in the much less hurried atmosphere of Middle Park. The ski slopes of Winter Park, Mary Jane, and SilverCreek combined with Rocky Mountain National Park, Indian Peaks Wilderness Area, Lake Granby, Shadow Mountain Lake, and Grand Lake give Snow Mountain Ranch guests unequalled year round recreational opportunities.

Camp Chief Ouray provides a resident camping experience steeped in the traditions of YMCA camping. Each year 1,500 youth and 275 adults enjoy an experience unique to resident camping.

Snow Mountain Ranch's 85 kilometers of nordic trails are unequaled.
YMCA of the Rockies

Camping at Snow Mountain Ranch.
YMCA of the Rockies

Colorado Dance Camp works out in the Kiva building at SMR.
YMCA of the Rockies   Carl Scofield

Games at Estes Park Center's Day Camp.
YMCA of the Rockies   Carl Scofield

YMCA guests rafting on the Colorado River.
YMCA of the Rockies

A family reunion enjoys roasting marshmallows.
YMCA of the Rockies   Carl Scofield

Hiking in Rocky Mountain National Park renews spirit, mind, and body.
Winter Park Photo   Grafton Smith

Epilogue:
A Glimpse Into the Future

A strong vision for tomorrow has been one of the guiding principles of the YMCA of the Rockies since the Grand Lake Encampment in 1907. Even in times of trouble the Association looked ahead. The future as envisioned in the following pages is a combination of fact and dreams derived from preliminary discussions between Board and staff. In an uncertain world some dreams may take decades to fulfill. Some may never come to fruition.

In May 1990 the YMCA of the Rockies began building its vision of tomorrow. Campaign for Our Future targeted four areas of need including: renovation of the Administration Building at Estes Park Center, a new dining and conference facility at Snow Mountain Ranch, a new family program center at Estes Park Center, and continued renovation of cabins.

The Administration Building has been an Estes Park Center landmark since 1910, and it has witnessed many changes through the decades. Built as a summer only building, it is not properly winterized. It needs extensive renovation to continue meeting the Association's needs into the next century. Plans call for the work to be completed in two phases.

Phase I includes a complete updating of all mechanical systems, insulation, new roof, thermal windows, and extensive structural repairs. The existing west end housing the Rustic Room will be removed and a new wing added to house a snack bar, grocery, and gift shop. The space now occupied by the gift shop will be turned into a lounge area. The addition requires removal of the Post Office/Grocery Store building. The Post Office will possibly move to the lower level of the Walnut Room. In Phase II the entire bathhouse addition built in 1924 will be removed and replaced with modern office space for Estes Park Center staff. Both Phases will be completed when and if the necessary funds are raised.

The existing dining rooms and kitchen at Snow Mountain Ranch have been inadequate for years. The kitchen is often stretched beyond capacity serving large conference groups downstairs while providing restaurant service to vacationing families in the Aspen Room. A challenge grant of $500,000 was pledged by the Schlessman Family Foundation for this facility. The pledge is contingent on the Association raising the remainder of funds from various sources. The proposed Schlessman Conference and Dining Center will be located on the knoll behind Aspenbrook and Silver Sage Lodges. The building will include dining facilities for 600 people and meeting space for a like number. When all kitchen and dining facilities are relocated to the Schlessman Conference and Dining Center, the current kitchen and three dining rooms located in the Administration Building will be remodeled into conference, meeting, and office space.

The need for an adequate program auditorium has been recognized for many years at the Estes Park Center. The Walter G. Ruesch Auditorium is booked most of the busy summer season by large conferences, forcing program activities to meet in less adequate facilities. George and Elaine Hempel pledged a $125,000 lead gift to build the Hempel Family Program Center. It will include a 300 seat theater style auditorium equipped with the latest sound and lighting equipment as well as dressing rooms and offices. The auditorium will be used for a variety of family-oriented, cultural, and educational programs. Construction will begin in as soon as the remaining funds are raised.

As the YMCA of the Rockies looks into the next century, the Association has many other needs in order to fulfill its mission. The demand for cabins and lodge rooms at Snow Mountain Ranch far exceeds supply at peak times. At both Estes Park Center and Snow Mountain Ranch family reunion facilities are booked years in advance. Camp Chief Ouray has to turn away many girls because of inadequate space. At Estes Park, older buildings need to be replaced. Both centers need to move their support buildings to outlying areas to create a more pleasing environment for guests.

With completion of the 170 acre foot Gaylord Reservoir in 1991, a major obstacle for further development was removed. Renewed expansion of Snow Mountain Ranch began in 1992 with the opening of a new cabin area in the valley west of Aspenbrook and Silver Sage Lodges. Initially, twelve cabin sites are planned. Construction will begin in 1993 or when donors are found.

Several other projects are projected within the next ten years at Snow Mountain Ranch. The current maintenance buildings will be torn down; maintenance operations will be moved to an out of the way location. After completion of the Schlessman Conference and Dining Center, there is a possibility that two new lodges will be built to complement the complex.

With family reunion facilities at Snow Mountain Ranch filled at peak season, new family reunion accommodations need to be constructed. One possible location is a site overlooking the Pole Creek meadow near current family reunion cabins.

At the Estes Park Center, building for the future started in 1992 with complete renovation of Alpen Inn. At the same time, the YMCA will also build a new accommodation carrying the historic name, Wind River Lodge. Located on the hill behind Alpen Inn and Mt. Ypsilon Lodge, Wind River Lodge will have 100 rooms. In the lower level there will be three meeting rooms for 100 persons each.

Construction of Wind River Lodge will allow the eventual release of Hallets, Howard, and Hague for staff housing. The next step will include redevelopment of the area now occupied by staff housing and maintenance. The process was initiated in the spring of 1992 when the old Housekeeping building was torn down. Eventually, Chapin, Pioneer, Fern-Odessa, and Maintenance will be razed as well. The surrounding staff houses will be relocated to the perimeter of the grounds or torn down.

If funds are available, Mt. Ypsilon Lodge will be completely remodeled in 1993. Before the turn of the century, three of the Eastside lodges, Twin Sisters, Rainbow, and Deer Ridge will require extensive renovation or replacement.

On the Second Mesa, the "Japanese Indian" cabins will be razed as donors are found to replace them. Other existing two bedroom cabins will continue to be updated through the cabin adoption program. A smaller but similarly equipped family reunion lodge will be built either west or south of Pattie Hyde Barclay Reunion Lodge.

The fate of historic Mountainside Lodge has Board and staff in a dilemma. Unless a major contributor is found for a total restoration of the building, it will have to be razed. If it is razed, it is hoped that the beautiful stonework can be incorporated into the new structure.

As the Estes Park Center has grown over the years, the original Dining Hall has been added on to, remodeled, and adapted. The resulting complex is inefficient and antiquated. Consequently, it will require complete renovation or replacement.

Many guests feel that programming is the single most important feature that sets the YMCA of the Rockies apart from other resorts and conference centers. Programs at both Snow Mountain Ranch and Estes Park Center will continue to emphasize the needs of families. While each center will develop programs to meet the needs of its particular communities and constituency, there is common agreement as to the direction programming will take in the next century.

Programs in the future will continue to stress serving the total person by helping the individual to develop in mind, spirit, and body. Activities will continue to put an emphasis on the family unit through programs such as Daddy Day and Family Olympics. The Program Departments at both centers will seek to develop activities that educate participants while entertaining them. Guests will see more programs commonly associated with their hometown YMCAs allowing them to initiate or continue programs participated in at home. To serve their surrounding communities Snow Mountain Ranch and Estes Park Center will develop programs to provide a break from long winters in the mountains.

The destiny of the YMCA of the Rockies during the next century will be determined by geopolitics, weather, changing constituency, and an unknown number of other factors. Whatever the next century holds, the YMCA of the Rockies will be guided by its mission of serving families, conferences, youth, and staff in a Christian environment.

Presidents of the
Board of Directors: 1907-1992

William E. Sweet
Clarence P. Dodge
Ira E. Lute
Albert A. Hyde, Emeritus
W. C. Coleman, Emeritus
Ralph B. Mayo
Lewis A. Dick
Elmer Magee
Herbert O. Willborn
Dwight L. Dannen
James R. Bellatti
Herbert C. Kroeplin
Flavel Simcox

Members of the
Board of Directors: 1907-1992

George H. Ahlborn
B. G. Alexander
Karl Amelang
J. D. Anderson
William T. Arnold Jr.
F. G. Atwood
J. P. Bailey
Brutus Baker
Burke Baker
Steadman Ball
David Barclay
Pattie Hyde Barclay

C. A. Bartles
James R. Bellatti
Richard E. Bennett
Nelson W. Benning
Roy F. Bergengren
Dana X. Bible
Iver L. Bidne
Gus S. Bilheimer
Helen B. Bisgard
Carl S. Bishop
Louis A. Black
Robert P. Bogott

Alfred O. Booth
W. W. Bowman
E. Douglas Boyden
Orvill A. Boyle
Steve C. Brace
Earl W. Brandenburg
Fay E. Brainard
E. M. Braukman
E. M. Bray
Andrew C. Brethauer
Harry H. Broadhead
Theron Brown
C. E. Buchner
Frederick H. Bucholz
Urban Busiek
C. N. Cadwallader
Frank Cadwell
William L. Carter Jr.
W. Lee Carter III
R. M. Cawthrone
James H. Causey
Frank H. Cheley
Horace G. Christopher
Don Christy
S. H. Clammer
W. Dale Clark
Kenneth B. Clark
Fred P. Clatworthy
S. E. Cobb
W. C. Coleman
Ben L. Collins
Harold Colvin
L. A. Colter
Howard Cowden
Oscar L. Cox
S. Hugh Cronin
W. B. Culbertson
Ralph F. Curry
E. Guy Cutshall
Dwight L. Dannen
H. L. Dannen
George R. Davis
John W. Davis

W. H. Day
Thomas M. Deal
Russell Dearmont
F. M. Deerhake
E. F. Denison
Charles G. Dibrell Jr.
Lewis A. Dick
Clarence P. Dodge
Henry Dorsey Sr.
Dorothy Dreffin
H. B. Durham
Kenneth G. Eastman
C. V. Edgar
B. V. Edworthy
James F. Eggleston
Lester M. Ellis
August Epp
Herbert E. Evans
William S. Fallis
William Farha
William G. Farrington
Thurston Favor
C. H. Fenstermacher
Frank C. Fields
Haylor H. Fisher Jr.
Charles W. Fordyce
Randall Foster
George W. Fraiser
Roy O. Frantz
Ray F. Frey
William E. Friend
John W. Fuhrer
F. A. Garrison
E. K. Gaylord
Guy T. Gebhart
Cyrus S. Gentry
E. Wilson Germany
Harper Glezen
L. E. Goodwin
William J. Grede
Sam Greenland
W. E. Greer
Henry E. Grim

Charles B. Hall
C. S. Hamilton
Robert T. Harper
Hastings Harrison
Jesse L. Haugh
J. Clinton Hawkins
L. C. Hayworth
C. D. Hayes
Paul Hayward
Walter W. Head
Jack W. R. Headley
Philip Heckman
Harry L. Heinzman
R. W. Hendee
John H. Henry
Pat Henry Jr.
Patrick Henry
Rodney C. Hibner
Bruno Hobbs
Homer L. Hoisington
Leland L. S. Holdt
John G. Holland
Walter S. Hopkins
H. H. Horne
C. Earl Hovey
Louis F. Howard
Julie Hughes
John L. Hunter
Albert A. Hyde
George Hyde
Maurice Hyde
C. W. Jenness
Lothardt Jensen
A. L. Johnson
John R. Johnson
H. E. Johnson
Rick Johnson
E. V. Johnston
Larry A. Jones
Lem T. Jones
William D. Jordan
Richard Kane
George A. Kassabaum

Howard Kast
Ned Kemp
George Kessler
Lowell King
George M. Kirk
J. B. Kroffin
Herbert C. Kroeplin
Howard E. Kusterman
Drew H. Lander
R. S. Lander
George K. Landis
Robert B. Langworthy
Don A. Larsen
Charles M. Law
M. Stanley Lee
Georgia Legett
George E. Lerrigo
Wendel D. Ley
Joanne C. Linnes
Lowell C. Linnes
John R. Longmire
C. G. Lord
Dr. Charles A. Lory
W. A. Luke
W. E. Lusby
Ira E. Lute
Norman Macleod
Elmer E. Magee
Robert Magee
John E. Manley
Don L. Marketto Jr.
James Maston
William H. Maxant
A. L. Mayer
Charles M. Mayne
Ralph B. Mayo
William A. McAllister
Clarence B. McClelland
Eugene McCarthy
F. J. McConnell
J. J. McConnell Jr.
John D. McEwen
George McNeish

Sutherland Miller
W. W. Mills
A. B. Minear
Lee A. Moe
Harold W. More
William M. Moore
Earl A. Morgan
Clair K. Morris
Charles A. Musselman
John C. Naylor
David Neiswanger
L. S. Nelson
Raymond F. Nelson
Paul M. Newstrom
Van N. Nichols
David H. Nicholoson
Raymond Norman
D. C. Norwood
Rol Otis
W. C. Paige
Rodney D. Palmer
M. F. Palmer
Frank B. Parker
Donald Patterson
Herbert M. Peck
E. W. Peirce
J. Gordon Peterson
Clifford Pierce
Fred D. Pierce
R. C. Pifer
A. M. Piper
O. L. Plucker
David W. Pollard
Glen Preston
D. C. Proctor
W. C. Proctor
Charles Puelher
Frank A. Randall
A. A. Remington
F. B. Reynolds
I. B. Rhodes
J. Deen Ringer
W. R. Robbins

C. C. Roberts Jr.
George Roesler
Frank Sanders
Dean E. Schaffer
Lee E. Schlessman
W. G. Schmiederer
Sam J. Schreiner
Homer A. Scott
W. A. Scott
Albert Sechrist
Linwood B. Sexton
K. A. Schumaker
E. Ray Siler
Ivan J. Singleton
E. B. Simmons
Flavel Simcox
Clifford A. Smith
DeWitt I. Smith
Edgar A. Smith
W. Angie Smith
Roy Sorenson
J. E. Sprout
Ralph Squires
W. F. Stahl
Clare N. Stanard
Frederick L. Starrett
Albert Steves IV
Graham Stewart
Robert M. Stewart
Champe J. Stoakes
John L. Stone
John Timothy Stone
Charles M. Strader
William A. Sullivan
Gordon Sweet
William E. Sweet
William E. Sweet II
William E. Sweet III
Wayne R. Tatman
E. Taylor
Robert Timothy
Charles G. Titus
Waldo Toeves

Joseph C. Todd
W. B. Todd
L. A. Toothaker
Gavin Ulmer
W. B. Van Akin
E. D. Verink
Robert Vernon
Walter C. Veazie
C. I. Vessey
B. C. Wade
Robert E. Waite
G. R. Warner
Charles S. Watson
Dr. Wegner

C. R. Welch
Frank H. West
John C. Wharton
G. E. Whipple
J. B. White
V. M. Wiley
Herbert O. Willborn
Urban Williams
W. C. Williams
R. E. Wilson
William A. Wilson
J. B. Withee
Ralph Wood
Eugene P. Zachman

Chief Executives of the YMCA of the Rockies

A. G. Pearson
J. E. Congdon
Gus S. Bilheimer
Morris N. Dillon
Ira E. Lute
Lewis A. Black
A. A. Ebersole
Herbert Evans
A. L. Mayer
Lisle T. Ware
Bernhard Timmerman
Walter G. Ruesch
DeWitt I. Smith
Richard Protzmann
E. Eugene Garris

Managing Directors of The Estes Park Center

E. Eugene Garris
Gary Baxter

Managing Directors of Snow Mountain Ranch

James A Brigham
Richard M. Engle
Jerry Donner
Kent Meyer

About the Authors

While on a church youth trip in 1962, Jack Melton climbed Ram's Horn Mountain. The sea of red roofs that was the YMCA of the Rockies was overlooked in the excitement of the moment.

What was Lulabeth Cox doing that same day? She was probably at Day Camp or horseback riding in the National Park. Her family, the Dorseys, first visited the YMCA of the Rockies in 1917. Having been born into the YMCA family she spent every summer, except her first, there. In 1969 she introduced Jack to the YMCA. It was love at first sight. After marrying in 1974, the couple taught school in their native Dallas while spending their summers in Estes Park at the family cabin, Outlook. They hiked hundreds of miles in the National Park and surrounding mountains.

In 1979, Executive Director Walter Ruesch asked them to assist in establishing a museum at the Estes Park Center. Since they were partly responsible for Lula Dorsey offering to save a portion of the Wind River Lodge, they felt compelled to assist. It was also a chance to give something back to the Association which had enriched their lives.

Arriving in June 1979, they were greeted with an empty and unfinished building. With no specific qualifications and the naivete and brashness of youth, they dove into the project. After six weeks of work, the museum was ready for opening. What they had learned about the history of the YMCA in the short period of time whetted their appetite for more.

Suffering from urban burnout, the Meltons moved to Estes Park in August 1980. In 1981 they were asked to complete research for a 75th Anniversary publication. The history of the YMCA of the Rockies became a giant jigsaw puzzle with an unknown number of pieces. Several months of intensive research resulted in <u>YMCA Of the Rockies: Seventy-Five Years of History 1907-1982</u>.

During the ensuing years the couple spent their summers working at the Dorsey Museum while pursuing a variety of endeavors to make ends meet. In 1986, Lulie resumed her career as an educator with the Thompson School District in Loveland, Colorado. In 1987, Jack was hired by the YMCA on a full time basis. Today, he is the Membership Director and Information Systems Manager.

In the Fall of 1990, the Meltons decided that it was time to update the Association's history. During the following one and a half years, they retraced research completed in 1981 and pursued leads developed during the past ten years resulting in YMCA of the Rockies: Spanning a Century.

Today, the couple lives in Thunder Mountain Park, just minutes away from the Estes Park Center. They enjoy hiking, biking, birding, and rejoice in the privilege of living in Estes Park.

Bibliography and Suggested Reading List

YMCA of the Rockies history:

Hyde, John A. "A Balm in Gilead." Kansas History, Vol. 9, Number 4 (Winter 86-87), 150-163. (Story of Mentholatum and biographical information on A.A. Hyde).

Lula W. Dorsey Museum. Archives of the YMCA of the Rockies.

Melton, Jack R. and Lulabeth Melton. YMCA of the Rockies: Seventy-Five Years of History 1907-1982 . Estes Park, 1982.

Schreiner, Sam J. The Story of the Estes Park Conference. Estes Park, 1957.

Scroggs, Marilee Munger. A Light in the City - The Fourth Presbyterian Church of Chicago. Chicago, 1990. (Biographical information on Dr. John Timothy Stone).

YMCA of the Rockies. Board of Directors Minutes. Estes Park, 1907-1992.

YMCA of the Rockies. The Blue Mist: A YMCA of the Rockies Folktale. Estes Park, 1986.

Young, Rick. Rowley Homestead Museum and Nature Center. Winter Park.

YMCA history:

Binfield, Clyde. George Williams and the Y.M.C.A. London, 1973.

C. Howard Hopkins. History of the YMCA in North America. New York, 1951.

Shedd, Clarence Prouty. History of the World's Alliance of Young Mens Christian Association. London, 1955.

Turner, Eugene A. 100 Years of YMCA Camping. Chicago, 1985.

Witkay, Marie Helen. "Henry Franklin Kallenberg - Pioneer Physical Educator." Unpublished thesis. George William College, 1958.

Williams, J.E. Hodder. The Life of George Williams. New York, 1906.

Estes Park and Rocky Mountain National Park history:

Arps, Louisa Ward and Elinor Eppich Kingery. High Country
    Names. Estes Park, 1972.
Bird, Isabella. A Lady's Life in the Rocky Mountains. Norman,
    1973.
Buchholtz, Curt W. Rocky Mountain National Park - A History.
    Boulder, 1983.
Cotten, Don. ed. The Big Thompson Flood. Lubbock, 1976.
Mills, Enos. The Story of Estes Park. Estes Park, 1905.

Grand County history and skiing in Grand County:

Ciarns, Mary Lyons. Grand Lake in the Olden Days. Grand
    Lake, 1971.
Black, Robert C. III. ISLAND IN THE ROCKIES: The History
    of Grand County, Colorado to 1930. Granby, 1969.
Grand County Historical Association Journal. "A Mountain, A
    Dream, A Train-Winter Park." IX, Number 1. December
    1989.
Grand County Historical Association Journal. "Ranching and
    Ranchers: The Pioneer Breed." V, Number 1. February
    1985.

Index

Cover photographs:
Front: Courtesy Denver Public Library, Western History Department - L.C. McClure

Back: Lula W. Dorsey Museum